# A
# MOTOR RELEARNING PROGRAMME
# FOR STROKE

# A
# Motor Relearning Programme for Stroke

## Second Edition

## Janet H. Carr,

Dip. Phty, MA (Columbia)

*Fellow of the Australian College of Physiotherapists;*
*Senior Lecturer, School of Physiotherapy, Cumberland*
*College of Health Sciences, Sydney, Australia*

## Roberta B. Shepherd,

Dip. Phty, MA (Columbia)

*Fellow of the Australian College of Physiotherapists;*
*Senior Lecturer, School of Physiotherapy, Cumberland*
*College of Health Sciences, Sydney, Australia*

HEINEMANN MEDICAL BOOKS | ASPEN PUBLISHERS, INC.
Rockville, Maryland

Heinemann Medical Books
An imprint of Heinemann Professional Publishing Ltd
Halley Court, Jordan Hill, Oxford OX2 8EJ

OXFORD   LONDON   SINGAPORE   NAIROBI   IBADAN
KINGSTON

ISBN 0–433–05152–3 (UK edition)
ISBN 0–87189–312–6 (US edition)

First published 1982
Reprinted 1983, 1984, 1985, 1986
Second edition published 1987
Reprinted 1987, 1988, 1990

**US edition**

Distributed in Continental North America, Hawaii,
Puerto Rico and Canada by Aspen Publishers, Inc.

Printed in Great Britain by BAS Printers Limited,
Over Wallop, Hampshire and bound by
Butler and Tanner Ltd, Frome

# Contents

# *Preface to the first edition*

This book comprises a motor relearning programme (MRP) for stroke. In addition, some guidelines are given for establishing an environment which is conducive to learning and in which the person, following stroke, can make his best possible recovery of function. Appendices outline the factors which seem particularly essential for motor training, and indicate the theoretical mechanisms by which recovery may take place.

The MRP emphasises specific training of motor control in everyday activities, commenced as soon as the person's medical condition is stable. It represents a shift away from facilitation of movement and exercise therapy and involves specific training of muscle activity and functional movement of the affected limbs and the prevention of compensatory activity by either the affected or the intact side. The Programme's success depends upon the therapist training the patient to activate muscles in exactly the way they perform in normal everyday functions, monitoring his performance so the patient knows what he should and should not practise, preventing the habituation of incorrect motor responses. The techniques used require the patient to concentrate and to use his cognitive abilities, and side effects of the Programme have been improved concentration and cognitive function.

The development of this Programme represents the culmination of extensive literature research together with several years of clinical and teaching experience. We are aware of the need to research thoroughly the effectiveness of any new developments in physiotherapy, particularly since the therapeutic measures at present employed in stroke rehabilitation are carried out despite there having been little or no investigation of their effectiveness. In determining how to do this research, we had two objectives in mind. The first was to write out our treatment ideas in detail as a specific Programme so we would know exactly what we were researching. A problem in researching existing methods of treatment is their lack of detailed documentation. The second was to develop an assessment tool, since we considered that no existing instrument would adequately measure the most essential motor functions. We therefore set about the two tasks. This book is the result of the first. A motor assessment scale* for stroke which has been tested and found to have both inter-rater

*Carr J. H., Shepherd R. B., Nordholm L. and Lynne D. (1985). A motor assessment scale for stroke. *Physical Therapy*; **65**: 175–180.

reliability and test-retest reliability is the result of the second.

Our clinical experience and that of several colleagues using this Programme have been so encouraging that we feel justified in publishing the Programme before it has been researched. This research will commence with a series of single-person case studies. The MRP in its present state represents a beginning of what we consider will constitute a new direction in physiotherapy for the person with brain damage. It is our intention to continue the Programme's development as increasing knowledge and the results of research enable us to make changes and additions. We hope others will also be interested in developing these ideas further.

The MRP appears prescriptive in terms of the treatment or training given. However, the choice of movement components on which to concentrate, the monitoring of the patient's performance and the increasing of complexity will depend on the individual therapist analysing problems accurately and thoroughly and making the correct decisions. The individuality of patients is often used as a reason for not developing prescriptive programmes, for not researching treatment and to support the existence of many different treatment 'approaches'. However, although patients are indeed individuals, the basic motor needs of all humans are the same and our methods of learning motor skills have many common aspects. The existence of many different 'approaches' in stroke rehabilitation may indicate that none is truly effective and the idea that a variety of different approaches to treatment is advantageous or necessary is probably misleading.

We have not set out to write a complete book on stroke. The MRP represents the physiotherapist's contribution to the rehabilitation process in terms of motor training and, to be fully effective, the Programme will need to be combined with other planned programmes for stimulating mental, communication, visual and other functions. There should be easy access to medical care, psychiatric care and community resources. The patient must be in an environment in which motivation, positive attitudes, reinforcement from relatives and friends and consistency of practice are organised, not left to chance or to the goodwill of staff.

Extensive referencing has been included throughout the text in order that interested therapists and others may read the material which has helped us develop our theories and in order to encourage research into the many questions this Programme raises. Throughout the Programme, as in the rest of this book, the masculine pronoun refers to the patient and the feminine to the therapist, except in the captions to the photographs, when the pronoun will relate directly to the person photographed.

# *Preface to the second edition*

In our view, the physiotherapist is an applied movement scientist, clinical practice for the most part being developed from theoretical material in other disciplines. Our interest in writing both editions of this book has been to demonstrate how physiotherapists can derive clinical implications from theoretical and research material in the broad field of movement science, and to stress the necessity for this process to be ongoing.

We applied this new theoretical model for rehabilitation, which we have called a motor learning model, originally to stroke. However, the underlying theoretical assumptions, involving as they do aspects of motor control and motor learning, apply to any person with a motor disability who wants or needs to learn some particular motor task and to become skilled in it.

Any theoretical model and the clinical practice that follows from it should be in a continual state of development. The therapeutic model we proposed in the first edition of this book has stood the test of time rather well so far, in that most of the major theoretical assumptions concerning movement control, dyscontrol and recovery processes upon which it was originally based continue to be valid. However, our increasing knowledge about human motor behaviour in the fields of biomechanics, motor learning, neuroscience, cognitive psychology and human ecology has enabled us to update our theoretical rationale and some of the practical details of the Programme in this revised Edition. It is the chapters relating to postural adjustments or balance which in particular have been changed, since there have been significant developments in the study of postural adjustments in different contexts which have direct relevance to the clinic.

To train patients using this motor learning model, the therapist will need to read widely in the movement science field and the references and further readings included throughout the book would, we hope, provide an interesting and relevant study course.

# *Acknowledgements*

The authors wish particularly to thank David Robinson who took the photographs and Sue Ferris, assisted by Therese Adams, who typed the manuscript.

For their valuable comments and suggestions we wish to thank, in Australia, Louise Ada, Roger Adams, Ron Balnave, Colleen Canning, Dave Sanderson and Pippa Warrell; and in North America, John Basmajian, Leonard Diller, Richard Herman, Ron Marteniuk, Eric Roy, Shirley Sahrmann, Shirley Stockmeyer, Edward Taub, Paul Wang, and those masters, doctoral and post-doctoral students at Columbia University, New York and the University of Waterloo who gave their time and thought to discussing our ideas with us. Our grateful thanks go also to the people whose photographs appear throughout the text.

Figures 3.2 and 3.3 are from *Physiotherapy in Disorders of the Brain* (Janet H. Carr and Roberta B. Shepherd, 1980) published by William Heinemann Medical Books.

In conclusion, we would also like to express our thanks to the Principal of Cumberland College of Health Sciences, Dr Jeffrey Miller, and the College Council who granted us three months leave, and to Doreen Moore, the Head of the School of Physiotherapy, for her support and encouragement.

In preparing this new edition we have been assisted again by David Robinson who took the photographs, Sue Ferris who typed and retyped the manuscript, and Louise Ada and Colleen Canning, who read the manuscript and made valuable comments. Our thanks go to them and to the people who so kindly agreed to be photographed.

# PART I

# 1

# *Background to the development of the MRP*

Although stroke rehabilitation has to some extent progressed over the years, there is still a lack of enthusiasm in pursuing the goal of ensuring that each patient recovers his best possible function. The **quality** of rehabilitation must be questioned since much of it is based on theoretical assumptions that can no longer be easily supported, outdated ideas of exercise therapy, negative expectations, and on the passive notion of waiting for recovery to occur.

For these reasons the contribution of physiotherapy as expressed in the literature is still unclear. Some studies,[1,2] for example, have shown that the results following simple functional care are similar to the results following formal rehabilitation. One study[3] found that pain and stiffness in the shoulder developed more commonly in patients who received physiotherapy than in those who did not. Unfortunately, results from studies such as these detract from the potential contribution of physiotherapy following stroke.

Therapists still follow therapeutic concepts developed three decades ago, although these have never been developed and written down in a manner which enables them to be tested for effectiveness. Effort is expended in comparing these concepts and in developing an eclectic approach which can embrace all of them,[4,5] with the result that physiotherapy gives the appearance of looking backwards rather than forward, and of being more interested in justifying present techniques of treatment than in analysing motor problems and deriving clinical implications from theoretical research. Theoretical considerations still seem to depend solely on neurophysiological and medical data despite the advances in knowledge made by biomechanists and behavioural scientists. And, by and large, although many patients return home following stroke, the accepted norms in terms of motor function are walking deficiencies which require an aid of some sort and a non-functional upper extremity. In other words, the end result of a patient's lengthy rehabilitation process is frequently disabilities which may have been to some extent augmented by the very procedures intended to overcome these disabilities. The authors' clinical experience is that the end result of rehabilitation can be very different for many patients, but that this depends on physiotherapists recognising the real potential of physiotherapy as an applied movement science, dis-

3

carding no longer theoretically supportable methods, understanding the need to develop new methods of treatment based on updated theories of motor behaviour, researching their effectiveness and taking more responsibility for improving the general framework of stroke care.

**The unique contribution of physiotherapy to the rehabilitation of stroke lies potentially, in our view, in the training of motor control based on an understanding of the kinematics and kinetics of normal movement, motor control processes and motor learning.** For a number of years the authors have been working to develop what they consider should be the direction of modern rehabilitation, a major shift in emphasis away from exercise or facilitation therapy to the relearning of motor control; from a purely empirical role to an applied movement science role. This new direction has its origins in the work of the early pioneers in physiotherapy, who stressed the need to assist patients to gain their maximum functional potential. The authors of this book are appreciative of the roles of such pioneers as the Bobaths, Knott, Voss, Brunnstrom, Rood and others who developed their theoretical concepts and therapeutic ideas from the scientific knowledge of their time and as a result of their own observations. Working in the 1980s, one could be expected to look towards the scientific knowledge of *our* times and to derive clinical implications from this knowledge. To make our task a little easier, it happens that there has been an explosion of research in the field of neuroscience (particularly the movement sciences) which is more obviously relevant to clinical practice than much of the experimental work of the first half of the century.

The work of people such as Bernstein, Gibson, Gentile, Evarts, Kelso, Turvey, Nashner, Winter and Perry, to name just a few, provides, from their various fields of neurophysiology, biomechanics and psychology, experimental results and theoretical explanations based on studies of live awake animals and humans performing meaningful motor tasks. This is in marked contrast to early work in neurophysiology and psychology which involved experiments on isolated nervous systems and humans constrained to perform single joint movements.

As applied movement scientists, our task is to derive clinical implications from the work of scientists and theorists such as those referred to above, that is, to see the relevance of certain information and work out how to apply this information to the analysis of motor problems and to the training process (or, expressed from the patient's point of view, the learning process). A further task for the physiotherapist as applied movement scientist is to add to the knowledge of human movement in our time by investigating, or at least documenting and measuring, the motor behaviour of our disabled patients.

Emphasis in this new model is on practice of specific motor tasks, the training of controlled muscle action and control over the movement components of these tasks. Rehabilitation therefore involves the relearning of real-life activities, those which have meaning for the patient, and not facilitation or the practice of non-specific exercises.

Whatever one does in therapy reflects both implicit and explicit theoretical assumptions. Hence the therapeutic approaches of the past

30 years were based on certain assumptions about motor control, about dyscontrol and about recovery processes[6] which fitted the knowledge of the time.

The major assumptions about motor control underlying this new model are: (1) that regaining the ability to perform motor tasks such as walking, reaching and standing up involves a 'learning' process, and that the disabled have the same learning needs as the non-disabled (i.e. they need to practise, get feedback, understand the goal etc.); (2) that motor control is exercised in both anticipatory and ongoing modes and that postural adjustments and focal limb movements are interrelated; (3) that control of a specific motor task can best be regained by practice of that specific motor task, and that such tasks need to be practised in their various environmental contexts; and (4) that sensory input related to the motor task helps modulate action. These assumptions are based on what the authors know of current theories of movement and are in marked contrast to the assumptions underlying much current physiotherapy practice.

At present, physiotherapy for stroke varies not only from hospital to hospital but also from therapist to therapist within the same hospital, and this is no doubt one of the reasons why it is unusual to see the details of treatment written down and why the few studies done to evaluate effectiveness and outcome omit these details. Yet, if effectiveness is ever to be evaluated and if more appropriate methods of treatment are ever to enter into general use, treatment programmes must be described in detail. Of course, there are subtleties in physical treatment which are difficult to describe and some of these have to do with the therapist herself, her personality, her attitudes and her abilities. Physiotherapists have for too long used the fact that each patient needs individual treatment to excuse the lack of documentation of the outcome of treatment. Although treatment must take into account the needs of the individual patient, all stroke patients who have motor problems lack control over the essential movement components of activities such as standing up and walking, and therefore have the same basic motor needs. Experience with a large number of people following stroke has led the authors to the conclusion that it would be possible to design and write out a programme around a framework of these basic motor needs from which all patients would benefit, and which could be tested for effectiveness.

Compared with the prevailing rehabilitation attitudes, the motor relearning programme (MRP) may appear prescriptive. However, looked at closely it will be seen to depend upon the therapist's analysis of each patient's motor performance. The Programme provides *guidelines* for a training regime.

The Programme assumes the brain's capacity for recovery since it is dynamic and capable of **reorganisation and adaptation,** and that functional training (i.e. training of motor tasks) may in itself be remedial. It is assumed that the patient's experiences after his stroke (including his physiotherapy) will affect recovery processes either negatively or positively. Appendix 1 gives a brief outline of current theories of the mechanisms by which neural adaptation may take place.

The Programme is based on four factors known to be essential for the learning of motor skill and therefore assumed to be essential for the relearning of motor control following stroke: the **elimination of unnecessary muscle activity, feedback, practice,** and the **interrelationship between postural adjustment and movement.** Appendices 2 to 5 give some details relating to these factors.

A motor skill has been defined as 'any human activity that has become better organised and more effective as a result of practice'.[7] Everyday activities, even such apparently simple ones as standing up from sitting, therefore constitute motor skills. They occur through the activation of functional synergies made up of movement components which, when linked together in the appropriate spatial and temporal sequence, make up the controlled motor task. Some components appear more essential to the activity than others and are called **biomechanical necessities**[8] or **determinants**[9] as they are the key elements upon which the activity (and probably related activities) depends. Hence it is theorised that the patient needs to learn how to activate and control these specific components in the correct spatial and temporal sequence in order to be able to perform the task.

Relearning the everyday motor tasks contained in this Programme therefore involves the patient practising the tasks in which he was skilled before his stroke, helped by the therapist who instructs, explains, feeds back information and structures the practice environment. Where it is necessary for the patient to practise specific muscular activity, the therapist takes into account the apparent context-specificity of muscle action, something which traditional exercise therapy and facilitation techniques do not do. Muscles change their action (for example, from supination to flexion, from eccentric to concentric) depending on the initial position of the body part and the task which is being carried out.[10] A muscle may test strong at one length or for one task and be incapable of activation at another length or for another task. That is, relative activity of particular muscles differs in different actions.[11–13]

The mechanical response of a muscle to a neural signal appears to depend on the mechanical condition of the muscle at the moment the signal arrives. A motor activity is therefore affected by such peripheral factors as muscle length, velocity, temperature, joint angle, length of limb segments and external forces.[14] The warm-up phenomenon suggests that muscles may contract more efficiently after they have contracted a few times thereby producing heat. It is possible that the nervous system may be able to take advantage of certain muscle properties in order to use more easily generated neural signals to accomplish the desired result.[15] The aim in motor training is principally *muscle control*. That is, the therapist aims not merely at the activation of a maximum number of motor units unrelated to any specific motor task, but at helping the patient control the activity of the appropriate number of motor units for the particular task being retrained.

Necessary for all motor activity is the body's ability to **adjust to gravity** and therefore to **changes in body segment alignment,** so throughout practice of all activities, the therapist monitors the alignment of the body and the patient is trained to preserve a balanced alignment as he moves about. Appendix 5 gives some details related to normal balance.

Throughout the Programme, emphasis is on the patient consciously practising particular motor tasks, building up his awareness of his ability to elicit muscle activity and control movement, progressing to practice at a more automatic level in order to ensure that the task has been learned and skill therefore acquired. It is possible that the emphasis placed on cognitive function (that is, on thinking things through) and on learning[15] is itself an important stimulation to brain recovery. The authors' experience with people in the very early stages following stroke is that the stimulus to thinking provided by active participation in practice results in a marked and swift increase in alertness and motivation. Blood-flow studies[16,17] show that there is an increase in blood flow of approximately 20% when a subject is thinking.

If the patient is to learn, the rehabilitation environment must encourage the learning process. It is important that the therapist realises that a few correct performances of a task such as standing up, performed in the presence of the therapist, does not mean that the patient has learned how to stand up. Learning can only be assumed to have taken place when the patient can perform the task effectively and without thinking about it in a variety of different circumstances or contexts. A considerable amount of varied practice is required to enable the patient to learn the task. The therapist must take the responsibility for creating the right environment for learning and should liaise with the rest of the rehabilitation team in ensuring a positive milieu. These points are further elaborated in Chapter 2 of this section.

In order to use the Programme effectively, the therapist needs to develop her problem-solving skills. Problem-solving can be divided into five overlapping stages: recognition, analysis, decision-making, action-taking, and re-evaluation. Of these, the analysis and decision-making stages are probably crucial, and it is in these that most errors in therapeutic problem-solving occur.

Analysis of motor behaviour in the clinic takes place at several levels: behavioural, kinematic and kinetic, muscular and neural. At each level, analysis can involve both subjective observation and objective measurement. Throughout the MRP, guidelines are given to the clinician in terms of observational analysis and these guidelines result from the authors' understanding of the various tasks at each of the levels listed above. These guidelines will no doubt become clearer as more studies are done in which motor behaviour in both disabled and non-disabled subjects is measured at, for example, kinematic, kinetic and muscular levels.

Ongoing **observational analysis** of motor performance by the clinician provides the guide to the training process. **Measurement** of motor performance (that is, the quantification of motor performance) provides data on patient progress and effectiveness of therapy. It can be used for research, for record-keeping, and if displayed in the form of a graph, for example, for motivating the patient and therapist. Effective analysis depends upon the individual therapist's knowledge of movement. The therapist with a limited understanding of muscle action, for example, will be unable to make a correct analysis of motor tasks and this will result in inappropriate decisions about treatment which may not only be ineffective but may actually worsen the problems or initiate new ones.

Here are two examples of inadequate analysis leading to incorrect decision-making and therefore to inappropriate action-taking.

1. Difficulty stepping forward with the affected leg may be incorrectly analysed as being due to 'foot drop'. The patient may, as a result, be trained to hitch his hip during swing phase in order to clear his foot from the ground. However, difficulty clearing the foot from the ground during swing phase is usually due to a lack of knee flexion at toe-off and not to lack of dorsiflexion. Therapy should therefore be directed at training knee flexor activity at the particular point when it should normally occur (see p. 141).

2. Analysis may reveal that the patient has a lack of awareness of proprioceptive and tactile sensations on the affected side. If the therapist decides that movement difficulties are due principally to sensory dysfunction, she may commence the patient on a programme of sensory (usually tactile and proprioceptive) stimulation. This assumes that augmented sensory input will facilitate movement. It is likely, however, that afference is filtered so that only input relevant to a task is allowed through and unnecessary sensory input is inhibited. Following this assumption, a more appropriate decision would be to institute a motor training programme in which the patient has the chance to regain the ability to use sensory information (including visual) for its predictive function as well as for its regulatory feedback function.

However, a person who is regaining effective hand function may not be progressing in activities which require fine manipulation because of a degree of insensitivity at his fingertips. In this case, specific sensory acuity can be developed by, for example, practice of two-point discrimination, games involving recognition of texture and objects, as well as by practice in manipulating objects which require a fine degree of skill. In this case, the decision to include sensory training (specific experience, not generalised) may be more appropriate.

The effectiveness of the MRP depends to a large extent on the ability of the individual therapist:

- to keep abreast of developments in the movement sciences

- to analyse the patient's motor performance

- to explain clearly to the patient by speech and demonstration

- to monitor the patient's performance and give accurate and usable verbal feedback

- to recognise and discourage compensatory behaviour

- to re-evaluate throughout each session the effectiveness of her own and the patient's performance

- to progress the patient's level of performance as soon as he has grasped the idea of what he is practising

- to ensure a positive milieu with opportunity to practise throughout the day

- to provide an enriched environment in which the patient will be motivated towards recovery of both mental and physical abilities.

## REFERENCES

1. Feldman D. J., Unterecker J., Lloyd K., Rusk H. A. and Toole A. (1962). A comparison of functionally orientated medical care and formal rehabilitation in the management of patients with hemiplegia due to cerebrovascular disease. *J. chron. Dis*; **15**:297–310.
2. Stern P. H., McDowell F., Miller J. M. and Robinson M. (1971). Factors influencing stroke rehabilitation. *Stroke*; **2**:213.
3. Brocklehurst J. C., Andrews K., Richards B. and Laycock P. J. (1978). How much physical therapy following stroke? *Brit. med. J*; 20 May: 1307–1310.
4. Cocke M., Sawner K. A. and Scheer K. (1981). An integrated treatment approach to adult hemiplegia: Brunnstrom approach, neurodevelopmental treatment, proprioceptive neuromuscular facilitation technique. Unpublished paper delivered at *Annual Congress of APTA, Washington*.
5. Umphred D. A. (1985). *Neurological Rehabilitation*, Vol. III, Chs 1 and 4. St Louis: Mosby.
6. Held J. and Gordon J. (1984). Personal communication.
7. Annett J. (1971) Acquisition of skill. *Brit. med. Bull*; **27**:266–71.
8. Broer M. R. and Zernicke R. F. (1979). *Efficiency of Human Movement*, 4th edn. Philadelphia: Saunders.
9. Saunders J. B., Inman V. T. and Eberhard H. D. (1953). The major determinants in normal and pathological gait. *J. Bone Jt Surg*; **35A**, 3:543–58.
10. Evans W. F. (1976). *Anatomy and Physiology*, 2nd edn. New Jersey: Prentice-Hall.
11. Alexander R. McN. (1975). Evolution of integrated design. *Amer. Zool*; **15**:419–25.
12. Rasch P. J. and Morehouse L.E. (1957). Effect of static and dynamic exercise on muscular strength and hypertrophy. *J. Appl. Physiol*; **11**:29–34.
13. Sale D. and MacDougall D. (1981). Specificity in strength training: a review for the coach and athlete. *Can. J. Appl. Sports Sci*; **6**:87–92.
14. Partridge L. D. (1979). Muscle properties: a problem for the motor controller physiologist. In *Posture and Movement* (Talbott R. E. and Humphrey D. R. eds.) pp. 189–229. New York: Raven Press.
15. Rosenzweig M. R. (1980). Responsiveness of brain size to individual experience: behavioral and evolutionary implications. In *Development and Evolution of Brain Size: Behavioral Implications* (Hahn M., Jensen C. and Dudek B. eds.) New York: Academic Press.
16. Ingvor D. H. and Philipson L. (1977). Distribution of cerebral blood flow in the dominant hemisphere during motor ideation and motor performance. *Ann. Neurol*; **2**:230–37.
17. Yonekura M. (1981). Evaluation of cerebral blood flow in patients with transient attacks and minor strokes. *J. surg. Neurol*; **15**:58–65.

# FURTHER READING

Evarts E. V. and Tanji J. (1976). Reflex and intended responses in motor cortex pyramidal tract neurons of monkeys. *J. Neurophysiol*; **39**:1069–1080.

Gibson J. J. (1977). The theory of affordances. In *Perceiving, Action and Knowing: Towards an Ecological Psychology* (Shaw R. and Bransford J. eds.) pp. 67–82. Hillsdale, NJ: Erlbaum.

Gibson J. J. (1979). *The Ecological Approach to Visual Perception*. Boston: Houghton-Mifflin.

Kelso J. A. S. (ed.) (1982). *Human Motor Behavior. Hillsdale, NJ*: Erlbaum.

Whiting H. T. A. (1979). Input and perceptual processes in sports skills. In *Psychology and Sport* (Glencross D. J. ed.) pp. 22–47. Sydney: McGraw-Hill.

Whiting H. T. A. (1980). Dimensions of control in motor learning. In *Tutorials in Motor Behavior* (Stelmach G. E. and Requin J. eds.) pp. 537–50. New York: North Holland.

Whiting H. T. A. (ed.) (1984). *Human Motor Actions. Bernstein Reassessed*. New York: North Holland.

# 2

# *Creating an environment for recovery and for learning*

The purpose of rehabilitation should be to provide an environment for the patient in which he can learn how to regain motor control, reasoning ability and social skills. The MRP will have its maximum effectiveness if it is part of a rehabilitation environment in which there can be consistency of practice and the opportunity for personal development. In this chapter the authors suggest the conditions which are probably necessary for learning to take place, which will best stimulate the brain to adapt and re-organise and which will ensure generalisation and transfer of training from the rehabilitation setting into everyday life. Insufficient consideration has been given in the past to the need to provide an environment for learning. It is probable that some of the failure of modern rehabilitation for stroke is due to the impoverished, non-challenging environment in which many patients find themselves. The implication of training as described in this Programme is that the circumstances are organised to produce the most rapid improvement in skill possible.

## ADMISSION AND REFERRAL

'Stroke is a medical emergency which requires accurate diagnosis and optimum care and this can be best given in hospital.'[1]

Although there appears to be a great deal of evidence which supports admission to hospital and rehabilitation following stroke,[2-7] there are still many patients who are not admitted, whose relatives are expected to care for them at home. The stroke patient should have access to specialised diagnostic skill as well as to medical skill to reduce the incidence of complications, and this should apply as much to the elderly person as to a younger person. Without appropriate medical care an elderly person, who may otherwise have made a good recovery, may die as a result of neglect of a treatable medical problem, such as respiratory infection.

There are probably several reasons why many stroke patients are not referred for rehabilitation. Feigenson[8] includes the following in his list: many **physicians are reluctant** to treat vigorously elderly patients who have multiple medical problems; **physicians are frequently sceptical** about the effectiveness of rehabilitation on the problems following stroke; there is a **lack of facilities** adequately equipped for such rehabilitation.

11

The reasons for negative attitudes towards stroke amongst health professionals would be interesting to investigate. They may, for example, reflect pessimistic views about patient recovery following stroke expressed many years previously during undergraduate training.

The **cost of stroke rehabilitation**, which is high, may be another reason for non-referral, despite the fact that the cost of maintenance in the dependent state which may otherwise result is much higher.[9-11]

The effect of non-admission upon the patient and his family can be profound. Relatives can be so affected by the shock and struggle of the first few days that they may thereafter be unable and unwilling to cope with the situation. The shock associated with stroke is extreme, both for the patient and his relatives. Relatives often have great difficulty coping both emotionally and physically with the problems which arise. It may be impossible for inexperienced people to cope with their own stress as well as with the patient's stress reactions. It may also be impossible for a relative to care physically for the patient, that is, to wash and toilet him, to sit him up and to get him out of bed. The patient's feelings of helplessness and dependence are aggravated by this situation, whereas admission to an appropriate hospital unit is reassuring in its obvious provision of skilled care.

## STROKE UNITS

Several authors[12-17] support the idea that patients following stroke should be admitted to a stroke unit (a disability-oriented unit). Although there is in general an awareness that certain patients, for example the spinal cord injured, require specially trained nurses, medical practitioners and therapists, this awareness has not as yet extended to the stroke patient, who is still admitted to a general ward in the care of staff who have little understanding of his needs and, often, a pessimistic attitude towards his potential for recovery. This factor may be another reason for the poor result of rehabilitation.

It is unfortunate that many health professionals fail to appreciate the special needs of the stroke patient and, because of a lack of understanding of brain function, are unable to analyse his problems. Instead they may take the most obvious and superficial view of his behaviour. For example, if the patient does not do as he is asked he may be labelled 'difficult', 'unco-operative' or 'disoriented'. Analysis of his behaviour, however, may reveal that he has a unilateral spatial neglect, that competing auditory inputs with which he cannot cope result in an extinction of the input on one side, that he is profoundly depressed, and so on. A negative attitude towards the potential of people following stroke prevails in the medical, therapy and nursing professions. This is illustrated by the tendency to give custodial care rather than specific training based on the individual's need, and physical treatment based on ideas developed 30 years ago rather than treatment which takes into account recent advances in the movement sciences.

Stroke units have the advantage of concentrating staff skills and interests in a collaboration which ensures a better quality of patient care.[18] In a study[19] carried out in an attempt to determine whether or not stroke units can affect outcome, two groups of patients on similar therapeutic programmes were compared. The data showed that the stroke unit group, despite the fact that they had more medical problems and more severe neurological and functional deficits, were more likely to go home after treatment and walked better at the time they were discharged.

## THE QUALITY OF REHABILITATION

Whether or not rehabilitation is carried out within a regional stroke unit or a rehabilitation unit within an acute care hospital, it is the quality of rehabilitation which is important. There are several factors which affect the quality and therefore the outcome of rehabilitation. These include the following.

1. **An early start.** Rehabilitation should commence early,[11,18,20,21] as soon as the patient is medically stable, which is usually within 24 to 36 hours, and this should involve the patient getting out of bed and standing. There is evidence that good mental health is promoted by encouragement towards normal activities and interests,[22] and this encouragement should begin early in order to prevent a secondary mental deterioration. There are many physiological reasons also for an early start to rehabilitation, and these have to do with the brain's capacity for recovery (see Appendix 1). Stroke care begun late is inefficient and this inefficiency also adds to the cost of rehabilitation.[9]

2. **A rehabilitation plan.** This should consist of a general programme planned for all patients following stroke (involving, for example, encouragement of socialisation and communication), plus specific programmes planned to overcome particular problems.

The general programme is concerned with the way the patient spends his day, his milieu or surroundings. This ensures the provision of an appropriate environment in which the patient can be rehabilitated to his fullest potential. As soon as his vital signs are stable he should get up and dressed. Within the first week his day is planned to approximate to a normal routine: up in the morning; meals at a table with others; short nap in the afternoon; activities throughout the day, that is, times set aside for specific rehabilitation programmes and recreational activities; and to bed again, not in the late afternoon which is often the case, but at 9.00 or 10.00 p.m., following some after-dinner recreational activity.

Specific programmes are planned for each person's needs, and may include a motor training programme with the physiotherapist, and a self-care programme (including dressing) with the occupational therapist. The speech pathologist will plan the means by which communication can be established and stimulated in a dysphasic patient. The psychologist will plan programmes for overcoming specific visual problems, problems of neglect or of mental functioning. General relaxation training may need to be organised for the anxious or tense person.

The patient should be doing something physically and mentally for most of the day and must not spend long periods doing nothing, in isolated or depressing surroundings. Restriction of activity is known to cause impaired intellectual functioning.[23,24] The patient's day is planned, therefore, to avoid both disorientation in time and place, and helplessness.[25] Activities are planned carefully so they are enjoyable and not passive or meaningless. They should stimulate cognitive functioning and require from the patient responses to challenges similar to those he would normally receive in daily life. For example, he should be given the responsibility for keeping his various appointments. He should also take an active part in the planning of his daily programme, stating his preferences and actually helping with the organisation.

Staff should not see themselves as merely providing custodial care but should organise actively an environment which facilitates the patient's return to normal life. Relatives, friends or volunteer helpers[26] should be involved as they will very often be more successful than health personnel at thinking of activities which simulate normal life and therefore which give the patient something familiar with which to grapple.

3. **Consistency of practice.** Time spent in individual therapy sessions without further practice throughout the rest of the day should be considered as time wasted. Similarly, different and contradictory methods of rehabilitation will not only be confusing but will actually *prevent* the patient from regaining effective motor behaviour.

Motor learning requires the opportunity for practice and, as a general rule, skill in performance of a task increases as a direct result of practice. Consistency of practice is, however, a difficult point to establish in rehabilitation. For example, if the therapist is training the patient to stand up, the patient's goal will be to bring his shoulders forward in front of his feet as he pushes down through his feet and stands up. However, he will only learn to do this and develop skill standing up in a variety of contexts if he is able to practise this way outside therapy sessions. He will have a natural tendency to stand up using only his intact leg because of difficulty controlling his affected leg, and if the nursing staff, for example, reinforce this way of standing up, by telling him to push down on the arm of the chair and pivot on his intact leg, there is a high risk of the two methods becoming confused so that an inappropriate routine is learned. Consistency of practice requires that, in early rehabilitation, the patient is 'drilled' to perform the components of a task in their correct sequence with assistance and guidance so he learns the 'general rules' of the task he is relearning.

Unfortunately, in the attempt to help the patient achieve early independence, staff may encourage ways of achieving particular objectives which may actually prevent him from regaining real independence. As another example, a person who is encouraged to propel a wheelchair with his intact limbs may gain 'independence' of a sort. However, this activity also encourages non-use of the affected side, which will probably prevent the regaining of motor control in the affected limbs and eventual attainment of *real* independence.

4. **Motivation.** One of the objectives for the physiotherapist is to plan an enriched physical and emotional environment which will motivate the patient towards recovery. There is evidence that an enriched environment may play a significant part in recovery from brain damage.[24,27,28] Motivation needs to be organised. It may be lacking if the patient is fearful, anxious, apathetic or depressed. To benefit from and be involved in his rehabilitation programme the patient must be able to learn and it is well known that little learning takes place in the absence of motivation. Many stroke patients need closer personal contact with staff than is usual in the hospital or rehabilitation setting in order to participate fully in their treatment programmes.

The patient needs to be involved in the planning of his treatment and in the discussion of treatment goals. The weekly timetable should be discussed and written up in consultation with the patient and his relatives. The plan should appear to be achievable to the patient, with goals that are understandable and immediately relevant to his needs. He is encouraged to see his goals as the learning of tasks not as the practice of movements for their own sake.

On the whole, training will not be effective unless there is a feeling of need for or desire to learn the particular task involved. The patient may have a low expectation and may, during his stay in hospital or in the rehabilitation setting, become satisfied with a relatively low level of achievement, a lower level than he could actually achieve with a little more effort, application and improved self-concept. In a sense, the rehabilitation environment does not prepare the patient for life outside the institution. Few demands are made on him and, with help at hand, food prepared and served and a wheelchair provided, he finds he can do what he has to.

Another attitude which needs to be considered and discussed with the patient is that of 'time the great healer', that if he is patient, over a period of time he will improve. Unfortunately, this is not necessarily true, and this attitude needs to be changed so the patient will put his best efforts towards an active participation in the training process soon after his stroke rather than passively waiting for recovery to occur.

All patients following stroke have two major objectives—to walk and to use both hands. Part of the effectiveness of the MRP may be attributable to the motivating effect of its emphasis on directly training the patient for these tasks, in contrast to exercises and activities which are assumed by the therapist to carry over into function but which have no apparent relevance.

To make the best possible recovery, the patient will need to have people around him from whom he can draw courage. Staff who are stuffy, silent, aloof or too protective may actually prevent the patient from tapping his personal resources.[29] He needs reassurance, encouragement and proof of his capacity gradually to overcome the barriers with which he is surrounded.[22] Belmont and his co-workers[30] comment that brain-damaged patients probably require unique motivating conditions for performance and point out that this has received too little consideration. Motivation can also be provided by success, reward, by positive reinforcement such as praise or an attitude of pleasure, and by receiving immediate feedback of performance.

**Success** in treatment sessions counteracts the tendency towards depression following stroke[31] as well as leading to a more rapid development of skill. The effective therapist ensures that the patient achieves the set goal, by monitoring his performance and giving him guidance when necessary, and by ensuring that he does not persistently attempt something he cannot do. In order for him to recognise whether or not his attempts have been successful, it is important that the physiotherapist does not continually do the movement for him, that is, move him about passively. In general it appears that motivation is low when subjects are not able to make mistakes during practice,[32] and it is of course only by actively performing a task or part of a task that the patient is *able* to make errors.

The authors' clinical observations indicate that success is particularly important in the early stages of relearning a motor task as it increases the patient's level of aspiration. The therapist should scale, graph or videotape the patient's performance so he can see his improvement and have proof of his progress. The Motor Assessment Scale[33] can be used for this purpose.

**Positive reinforcement** is given through praise, affection and acceptance. The therapist should think carefully about the impact of praising a performance so that the patient can relate words of praise, such as 'good', to success. 'Good' is offered as a **reward** and not said automatically and without meaning. If he is not successful, the therapist can use other words or gestures in order to encourage him and to acknowledge his efforts. Praise as a direct reward is only effective if it is offered for accomplishment of some specific desired behaviour. It loses its impact if given lightly with no relationship to success.

**Social isolation** can affect the outcome of rehabilitation by affecting motivation. Hyman,[34] following an examination of the literature for some possible links between social isolation and poor performance in rehabilitation, lists ten hypotheses. These include: dissatisfaction with the pre-morbid life situation; the seeking of substitute social satisfaction in the treatment centre; lack of social support; absence of an advocate; recent bereavement; a low level of pre-morbid functioning.

If a patient appears unmotivated, the cause of this should be investigated. A patient's behaviour is a consequence of the limitations imposed on him by the damage to his brain, which results in disturbances of body responses, perceptual and thinking processes, a slowness in registering and retaining recent information, an inability to give proper language expression to what he does perceive, combined with emotional turmoil.[18] He may have difficulty grasping all aspects of a task or sorting out the essentials of a problem. The dysphasic person may have difficulty shifting mentally from one idea or topic to another. However, it should be noted that a lack of understanding both of a patient's behaviour and ways of remediating his problems may result in a patient being incorrectly labelled as lacking in motivation and this will result in failure to take the necessary action.

The **environment to which the patient can expect to return**, his **personality, drive, intellectual ability** and **expectations** are all major determinants of outcome as they will influence motivation.[18] The therapist requires an understanding of all these factors for each patient so that the programme which is planned will tap his individual resources and attributes, in other words, take advantage of his strengths and not emphasise or reinforce his weaknesses.

5. **Mental stimulation.** Although many patients eventually return to full mental capacity following stroke, it is certain that not enough time and thought are spent on the retraining of cognitive skills. A study done by Kinsella and Ford[35] showed insignificant improvement in intellectual competence in a small group of patients over a period of 12 weeks, although improvement was made on the other measured parameters, such as functional movement. Although, as the authors comment, this result could be attributed to the insensitivity of the tests or the size of the group, it is also probable that, where there are problems of intellect, improvement will not occur without specific training.

For the first few weeks after stroke, many patients describe a feeling of slowness in thinking and a difficulty with concentration. They may be aware of a difficulty with organisation of their thoughts. It has been suggested[36] that brain responses are slowed because of the asynchronous activity of the two hemispheres. Certain factors may accentuate the above problems and should be considered in rehabilitation. The 'isolated' patient, that is, the dysphasic patient, the patient left in bed 'to rest', left to sit alone, or placed beside a television set which he cannot see or control, begins to experience intellectual regression. Illness and certain drugs can also have a profound effect upon intellectual function and alertness, especially in elderly people.[37] Drowsiness and inability to concentrate may be the result of drug therapy and the rehabilitation team should question the necessity for such medication.

Removal from his habitual environment, particularly in the presence of communication problems, can have a similar effect, and the presence of relatives and the organisation of his day to simulate a relatively normal day may therefore make a marked difference to the patient. The rehabilitation team must be careful not to assume that the depressed, labile, confused patient has permanent cognitive impairment, and should set about analysing these problems just as they would analyse the physical problems.

Some patients have problems with memory and with cognitive functions which may be related to memory. These may be specific and involve an inability to recognise faces, or they may be represented by an inability to remember significant events, dates or places, or an inability to remember motor tasks which were practised the previous day. Specific memory training may be helpful for such patients. It is probable, however, that the inability to remember the day-to-day activities of the rehabilitation unit frequently represents the fact that no significant events occurred, that nothing that occurred was actually memorable and that, with no daily timetable or regularity upon which to fix an event, one day has merely merged with the next. More knowledge of how a patient actually spends his day[38] would probably explain his inability to remember.

Old age is sometimes considered to be the reason why a patient is slow to learn. However, a study[39] has shown that both aged and brain-damaged patients appear to have learning potential that does not differ from the younger subjects except for a time factor and a greater need for positive reinforcement. Old age in the chronological sense should not be considered as a barrier to rehabilitation.[11] Gersten[40] reviews some of the literature which examines the relationship between age and outcome of rehabilitation and he concludes that, whatever the relationship, it appears to be mediated by self-concept, family support and social activity.

Early experience of erect positions (sitting and standing) stimulates mental alertness. The MRP provides cognitive stimulation by demanding the patients participation and involvement and by its emphasis on the cognitive phase of learning. However, many patients should also participate in a **mental stimulation programme** planned by a psychologist and designed to help the person organise his thinking, and to retrain specifically those cognitive and perceptual abilities with which he has problems.

6. **Educational programmes.** An education programme for relatives and patients should include some lectures and group discussions on the pathophysiology of stroke, the meaning of symptoms, the adaptability of the brain, the physical and emotional effects of stroke, ways of communicating with the person who is dysphasic, planning for discharge, and family and community participation in rehabilitation.

One study[41] to assess the benefit of educational programmes for the patient and his relatives showed support and approval, and another study[42] showed that rehabilitation gains were maintained as well through education of the family as through the use of community services. This latter study also showed an increase, compared with similar studies done in 1958 and 1963, in accepting attitudes of both the rehabilitant and a significant family member. A survey[43] of family members following an educational programme showed decreased anxiety about stroke as well as more effective involvement in the rehabilitation process.

Relatives should be helped to see the significance of their support in helping the patient regain his self-esteem. They will also gain an understanding of the patient's problems through discussion with the rehabilitation staff and by actually participating in treatment sessions. This will motivate them towards carrying out recommendations. If relatives do not know what the patient is accomplishing in therapy, they will expect a lower level of performance at home.[44] They are, if they are educated from the onset of rehabilitation, being prepared for the patient's return home.

Relatives are, in most cases, untapped resources. If the therapist involves them in treatment from the onset, they will be able to give the patient opportunities for practice outside therapy hours. Lack of participation by relatives may result in them being fearful of their ability to cope once the patient goes home. The patient for his part will be motivated by the knowledge that the members of his family feel confident in their role and that he is not necessarily seen by them as a burden. Some suitable publications for patients and their relatives are listed at the end of this section.[26,29,45–47] The list includes articles and books by patients themselves.

An in-service educational programme for staff will enable the physiotherapist to explain how she teaches a patient everyday tasks such as standing up and walking. Not everyone will be teaching him these activities, but each will need to understand how best to help him to practise. This is particularly important for nursing staff, aides and assistants, who are in constant contact with the patient but whose job should not be to teach him how to move again but to give him the chance to practise correctly and know what to reinforce. All members of the team need to know how much assistance to give the patient, otherwise he may be left to struggle on his own or he may be given so much help that he is relatively passive. The patient can update this information as he improves or it can be written in a notebook which the patient keeps with him. Other members of the team will thus be able to reinforce throughout the day what the patient is learning and give him the **opportunity to practise, to achieve mastery and to transfer what he has been learning in training sessions into his everyday life.** Similarly, the speech pathologist will advise other members of the team on the best ways of communicating with the person who is dysphasic and of reinforcing his attempts to speak.

Educational programmes should also involve sessions aimed at helping staff understand the reasons for various types of behaviour demonstrated by stroke patients and ways of creating the best possible environment for recovery. Isaacs[18] comments that dissemination within the team of practical information about stroke is a most important aspect of rehabilitation. Feigenson[8] adds the point that successful rehabilitation requires organisation within the team, co-ordination of the patient's programmes and the ability to keep everyone inspired.

Two problems which the patient may suffer early after his stroke, and which need particularly to be understood by staff and relatives, are **outbursts of weeping** and **urinary incontinence.**

**Weeping,** which is distressing for patient, relatives and staff, represents a lack of physical as well as emotional control and the patient needs constructive help (see p. 82), a strategy to help him regain control, rather than expressions of sympathy. The therapist who does not understand the reasons for this weeping may make an inappropriate response, suggesting, for example, that treatment be postponed until the next day 'when he is feeling better'.

Many patients immediately following stroke experience some urinary and bowel **incontinence.** This is very embarrassing and will increase the person's already high level of anxiety. This state of affairs will be reinforced by constant reference by the staff to his incontinence. Certain factors add to the possibility of having an accident: the person with communication problems will have difficulty making his needs understood; the use of a pan or bottle in bed normally requires use of both hands and reasonable balance and agility, neither of which the patient has.

The patient needs reassurance that he will quickly regain control of bladder and bowel. If he has a communication problem, a way of telling the staff that he wants to go to the lavatory should be established. Staff should ensure that the patient who needs to re-establish control does not have to wait for assistance. He should use a commode rather than a bed pan. Catheterisation should be avoided as it is detrimental to the person's psychological well-being and may provoke urinary tract infection and encourage dependence rather than the gaining of control.

However, the most essential factor in regaining control is the early assumption of the upright position and movement within this position. Standing and moving about in standing will quickly enable the patient to regain control. Incontinence should not be allowed to interfere with or delay treatment, and accidents can be avoided by ensuring that the patient goes to the lavatory before his treatment sessions and at regular intervals throughout the day. Hospital staff should be aware that incontinence is often only a manifestation of the patient's inability to wait or his difficulty communicating his needs. Persistent incontinence should be investigated by a urologist.

7. **Planning for discharge.** Preparation for returning home involves a home visit by a therapist to assess whether or not any adaptation of the house is necessary, and a weekend leave from the rehabilitation unit. Although the authors' clinical experience indicates that the majority of patients do well when rehabilitation is appropriate, some patients will not regain independence, and will require organisation of domiciliary services, such as meals on wheels, home help, or a visiting nurse. The patient with restricted mobility should have access to a list of shops and other buildings free of architectural barriers. An introduction to a Stroke Club,[46] where patients and their relatives can express and share difficulties and experiences and participate in social activities, will help the patient develop social and personal confidence and make easier his return into the community. A member of the rehabilitation team should visit the patient in his home after he has returned home to see if he is maintaining his level of performance, to solve any unforeseen problems and to ensure that the patient is happy, active and still improving. Further consultation with a physiotherapist can be arranged if necessary through the Stroke Club.

**Physical fitness.** There are a variety of different ways of looking at the concept of efficiency of human movement[48] and a number of factors which affect it, including physiological, biomechanical, biochemical, psychomotor factors and others such as age, sex, level of skill learning and training. The concept of improving general fitness following stroke is on the whole ignored in the literature, although studies on physiological stress associated with functional tasks have shown physiological stress to be higher for stroke patients than for normal subjects.[49-51] Stroke patients may avoid certain activities, those which require higher energy costs because of fatigue, dyspnoea and weakness. This can result in depression, anxiety and further inactivity. Brinkman and colleagues[52] designed a conditioning programme over a 12-week period for stroke patients using a stationary bicycle. Subjects subsequently demonstrated improvements in both physical fitness and some aspects of self-concept. Both film analysis of several tasks and self-reports showed improvement in functional level (one man started to mow his lawn) in six of the seven subjects.

## MAJOR ENVIRONMENTAL FACTORS IN REHABILITATION

**Human ecology** is the study of the interrelationship of physical, social and psychological factors in the environment.[53] Other terms which have also been used to describe this discipline are social ecology, environmental psychology and ecological psychology.

The major theoretical and applied problems addressed in human ecology are how space and objects are used to mediate interpersonal relationships, how environments can be changed to influence behaviour, and the effect of such factors as institution size, crowding and an individual's sensitivity or susceptibility to environmental forces.

Although very little work has actually been done in rehabilitation settings, behaviour has been studied in a variety of therapeutic, educational and work environments including hospitals, nursing homes, schools, playgrounds and offices. These studies could provide a very interesting theoretical and practical framework for analysing and improving rehabilitation environments in terms of both the patient and worker. Ittelson and colleagues[54] suggested that an individual's behaviour within the environment is systematically related to the environment. It follows, therefore, that the environment can be designed to be a facilitator of desired behaviour.[55]

Barker used the term behaviour–milieu synomorphy to describe the close-fitting relationship between humans, objects and actions. He demonstrated that certain behaviour is demanded by certain settings.[56] This is a useful point for health professionals to keep in mind since there is often a tendency to attribute a patient's behaviour more to his stroke, personality or lack of motivation (that is, a person-centred view) than to his environment.

If Barker's concept of synomorphy is applied to a physiotherapy area (or an entire rehabilitation unit), it can be seen that the objects and persons fit, for the most part, compatibly together. This synomorphy may, however, mediate *against* the objectives of therapy. In this special, rather closed setting, patients hope to learn how to cope with the diversity of settings in the outside world. The fact that generalisation of a task, such as standing up, from therapy room to elsewhere in the rehabilitation unit frequently does not take place may indicate a major flaw in physiotherapy practice and the environment in which it is carried out. It is a common *cri de coeur* from therapists that a patient walks well in the therapy room but reverts to his limp as soon as he exits through the door. Willems[57] observed and systematically recorded the behaviour of several (spinal-cord injured) patients as they went from one hospital setting to another. He found that patients were much more independent and active in some settings, such as cafeteria and hallways, than in other settings, such as occupational therapy, recreational therapy and physiotherapy. He proposes that since the main objective is to train patients to be as self-sufficient as possible, programmes of therapy should be examined to learn why patients are relatively dependent and inactive in them. He suggests that one reason may be that staff are overly protective of patients.

The typical rehabilitation centre has been built to a medical or sickness/disability model in which the emphasis is on treatment. The 'patient' attends in order to *receive* treatment. As Keith[58] points out, referring to another systematic observational study (this time of stroke patients) in a rehabilitation hospital, the patient is in an ambiguous position: 'on the one hand he is subject to the restrictions inherent in a medically oriented regimen; on the other hand he is expected to participate actively in treatment in order to become as physically and socially competent as possible. A major goal of the organisation, to aid individuals toward functional recovery and independence, is often at cross purposes with the mode of service delivery set by professionals in which the patient has limited opportunity to exercise such competence for independence'.[58] In Keith's study, stroke patients were most frequently seen in solitary behaviour even though observations were made during a work day. Brodsky and Platt[59] also carried out a study of a rehabilitation unit which pointed out some of the ecological, professional and organisational problems associated with such a unit.

Canter and Canter[55] consider that failure in the establishment of learning environments can frequently be traced to inadequate definition of the overall goals. To identify as an objective the rehabilitation of patients following stroke is inadequate, offering little in the way of guidelines for establishing an environment for motor learning, social interaction and mental stimulation. As Canter and Canter express so clearly, 'what is necessary is a way of specifying therapeutic aims which enables the setting to be considered as a direct facilitator of those aims'.

Below is a summary of some of the factors in creating the right environment for the stroke patient.

1. If the patient is to make his best possible recovery from the effects of stroke, he should initially be in an environment in which he can receive effective diagnostic and medical care, an environment which reduces the likelihood of complications and motivates him. Once his vital signs are stable, he should move to a different environment, not medical or sickness oriented, but a health, fitness and learning oriented environment, planned around his greatest need which is to relearn motor tasks. This unit should be planned, with furniture and activities designed and staff selected for maximising practice of various tasks necessary for everyday life. The advantage of a specialised stroke unit is that all staff can be trained to bring this situation about. Criteria audit can be used to highlight particular problem areas and to assess the effectiveness of action taken to overcome problems. One such audit is reported by Truscott.[60]

2. Rehabilitation should commence within the first few days after stroke in order to prevent learned non-use of the affected side, disuse effects such as length-associated changes in soft tissues, muscle weakness, loss of endurance, and mental and perceptual deterioration, and to stimulate the patient's learning abilities in both motor and cognitive function.

3. Rehabilitation should consist of programmes specific to each patient's problems, and should include not only a motor programme, but also programmes designed to overcome his specific visual, cognitive and language problems. The patient's day should be planned in such a way that he is given practice in leading a 'normal' busy life, learning to take responsibility, to regain a sense of time, etc.

4. If patients are to be motivated to regain a normal capacity for life, such motivation must be planned and not left to the discretion of individual therapists.

5. Consistency between the training of tasks with the therapist and performance of these tasks with other members of the staff during the day must be ensured. This will encourage learning to take place.

## REFERENCES

1. WHO (1971). Cerebrovascular disease: prevention, treatment and rehabilitation. *Wld Hlth Org. techn. Rep. Ser*; 469.
2. Langton Hewer R. (1976). Stroke rehabilitation. In *Stroke* (Gillingham F. J., Mawdsley C. and Williams A. E. eds.) pp. 476–490. London: Churchill Livingstone.
3. Steers A. J. W. (1976). Immediate care of stroke. In *Stroke* (Gillingham F. J., Mawdsley C. and Williams A. E. eds.) pp. 263–273. London: Churchill Livingstone.
4. United States Department of Health Education and Welfare (1976). *Guidelines for Stroke Care*. Washington DC: United States Government Printing Office.
5. Weisberg L. A. and Nice C. N. (1977). Intracranial tumors simulating the presentation of cerebrovascular symptoms. Early detection with cerebral computed tomography (CCT). *Amer. J. Med*; **63**:517.
6. Brocklehurst J. C., Andrews K., Morris P. E., Richards B. R. and Laycock P. L. (1978). Why admit patients to hospital? *Age and Ageing*; **7**:100–108.
7. Mulley G. and Aire T. (1978). Treating stroke: home or hospital. *Brit. med. J*; **2**:1321.
8. Feigenson J. S. (1979). Editorial. Stroke rehabilitation: effectiveness, benefit and costs. Some practical considerations. *Stroke*; **10**:1–4.
9. Kottke F. J. (1974). Historia obscura hemiplegiae. *Arch. phys. Med*; **55**:4–13.
10. Lehmann J. F., De Lateur B. J., Fowler R. S. *et al* (1975). Stroke: does rehabilitation affect outcome? *Arch. phys. Med*; **56**:375–82.
11. Feigenson J. S., McDowell F. H., Meese P., McCarthy M. L. and Greenberg S. D. (1977). Factors influencing outcome and length of stay in a stroke rehabilitation unit. Part 1. *Stroke*; **8**:651–6.
12. Drake W. E., Hamilton M. J., Carlsson M. and Blumenkrantz J. (1973). Acute stroke management and patient outcome: the value of neurovascular care units. *Stroke*; **4**:933–45.
13. McCann B. C. and Culbertson R. A. (1976). Comparisons of 2 systems for stroke rehabilitation in a general hospital. *J. Amer. Geriat. Soc*; **24**:211–216.
14. Isaacs B. (1976). The place of a stroke unit in geriatric medicine. *Physiotherapy*; **62**:152–4.
15. Feigenson J. S. and McCarthy M. L. (1977). Guidelines for establishing a stroke rehabilitation unit. *N. Y. St. J Med*; August:1430–34.

16. Howard B. E. (1977). A Practical Approach to Care of the Acute Stroke Patient in a Community Hospital Setting. Unpublished paper given at the *53rd National Congress of APTA, St. Louis, Missouri.*

17. Garraway W. M., Akhtar A. J., Prescott R. J. and Hockey L. (1980). Management of acute stroke in the elderly: preliminary results of a controlled trial. *Brit. med. J*; 12 April: 1040–43.

18. Isaacs B. (1978). Stroke. Who cares? In *Textbook of Geriatric Medicine and Gerontology,* 2nd edn. (Brocklehurst J. C. ed.) pp. 201–220. London: Churchill Livingstone.

19. Feigenson J. S., Gitlow H. S. and Greenberg S. D. (1979). Disability oriented rehabilitation unit—a major factor influencing stroke outcome. *Stroke*; **10**:5–8.

20. Stern P. H., McDowell F., Miller J. M. and Robinson M. (1971). Factors influencing stroke rehabilitation. *Stroke*; **2**:213.

21. Anderson T. P., Bourestom N., Greenberg F. R. and Hildyard V. G. (1974). Predictive factors in stroke rehabilitation. *Arch. phys. Med*; **55**:545–53.

22. Robinson R. A. (1976). Psychiatric aspects of stroke. In *Stroke* (Gillingham F. J., Mawdsley C. and Williams A. E. eds.) pp. 490–504. London: Churchill Livingstone.

23. Bexton W. H., Heron W. and Scott T. H. (1956). Effects of decreased variation in the sensory environment. *Can. J. Psychol*; **8**:70–76.

24. Walsh R. and Greenough W. (eds.) (1976). *Environments as Therapy for Brain Dysfunction.* New York: Plenum Press.

25. Seligman M. (1975). In *Helplessness on Depression, Development and Death.* pp. 21–41, 180–188. San Francisco: W. H. Freeman.

26. Griffiths V. (1970). *A Stroke in the Family.* London: Pitman.

27. Rosenzweig M. R., Bennett E. L. and Diamond M. C. (1967). Effects of differential environment on brain anatomy and brain chemistry. *Proc. Amer. psychopath. Ass;* **56**:45–6.

28. Walsh R. N. (1981). Sensory environments, brain damage and drugs: A review of interactions and mediating mechanisms. *Int. J. Neurosci*; **14**:129–37.

29. Hodgins E. (1966). Listen: the patient. *New Engl. J. Med*; **274**:657–61.

30. Belmont I., Benjamin H., Ambrose J. and Restuccia R. D. (1969). Effect of cerebral damage on motivation in rehabilitation. *Arch. phys. Med*; **50**:507–11.

31. Kottke F. J. (1975). Neurophysiologic therapy for stroke. In *Stroke and its Rehabilitation* (Licht S., ed.) pp. 255–324. New Haven: Elizabeth Licht.

32. Johnson P. (1984). The acquisition of skill. In *The Psychology of Human Movement* (Smyth M. M. and Wing A. M., eds.) pp. 215–239. London: Academic Press.

33. Carr J. H., Shepherd R. B., Nordholm L. and Lynne D. (1985). A motor assessment scale for stroke. *Phys. Ther*; **65**: 175–80.

34. Hyman M. D. (1972). Social isolation and performance. *J. chron. Dis*; **25**:85–97.

35. Kinsella G. and Ford B. (1980). Acute recovery pattern in stroke patients. *Med. J. Aust*; 13 December: 653–66.

36. Belmont I., Karp E. and Birch H. G. (1971). Hemispheric inco-ordination in hemiplegia. *Brain*; **94**:337–48.

37. Linford Rees W. (1979). Rehabilitation in the elderly. *Biblthca Psychiat*; **159**:155–62.

38. Keith R. A. and Sharp K. W. (1980). Time use of stroke patients in three rehabilitation hospitals. *Arch. phys. Med*; **61**:501–503.

39. Halberstam J. L. and Zaretsky H. H. (1969). Learning capacities of the elderly and brain-damaged. *Arch. phys. Med*; **50**:133–9.
40. Gersten J. W. (1975). Rehabilitation potential. In *Stroke and its Rehabilitation* (Licht S. ed.) pp. 435–471. New Haven: Elizabeth Licht.
41. Medcalf T. E. and Vandiver R. L. (1980). Stroke forum. *Phys. Ther*; **60**:905.
42. Anderson E., Anderson T. P. and Kottke F. J. (1977). Stroke rehabilitation: maintenance of achieved gains. *Arch. phys. Med*; **58**:345–52.
43. Wells R. (1974). Family stroke education. *Stroke*; **5**:393–6.
44. Andrews K. and Stewart J. (1979). Stroke recovery: he can but does he? *Rheumatology and Rehabilitation*; **18**:43–8.
45. Carr J. H. and Shepherd R. B. (1979). *Early Care of the Stroke Patient. A Positive Approach*. London: Heinemann Medical.
46. Griffiths V. (1978). *Volunteer Stroke Scheme Handbook*. London: Chest, Heart and Stroke Association.
47. Saw R. (1981). *The One-fingered Typist*. Sydney: Wildcat Press.
48. Cavanagh P. R. and Kram R. (1985). The efficiency of human movement—a statement of the problem. *Med. & Sci. in Sports & Exercise*; **17**:304–308.
49. Hirschberg G. G. and Ralston H. J. (1964). Energy cost of stair climbing in normal and hemiplegic subjects. *Am. J. Phys. Med*; **44**:165–8.
50. Corcoran P. J., Jebsen R. H., Brengelmann G. L. *et al.* (1970). Effects of plastic and metal leg braces on speed and energy cost of hemiparetic ambulation. *Arch. phys. Med. Rehabil*; **51**:69–77.
51. Landin S., Hagenfeldt L., Saltin B. and Wahren J. (1977). Muscle metabolism during exercise in hemiparetic patients. *Clin. Sci. mol. Med*; **53**: 257–69.
52. Brinkmann J. R. and Hoskins T. A. (1979). Physical conditioning and altered self-concept in rehabilitated patients. *Phys. Ther*; **59**:859–65.
53. Grannis J. C. (1985). Personal communication. Teachers College, Columbia University, New York.
54. Ittelson W. H., Proshansky H. M., Rivlin L. G. and Winkel G. H. (1974). *An Introduction to Environmental Psychology*. New York: Holt, Rinehart & Winston.
55. Canter D. and Canter S. (1979). *Designing for Therapeutic Environments*. Chichester: John Wiley.
56. Barker R. G. and Wright H. F. (1951). *One Boy's Day*. New York: Harper & Row.
57. Willems E. P. (1972). The interface of the hospital environment and patient behavior. *Arch. phys. Med. Rehabil*; **53**:115–22.
58. Keith R. A. (1980). Activity patterns of a stroke rehabilitation unit. *Soc. Sci. & Med*; **14A**:575–80.
59. Brodsky C. M. and Platt R. T. (1978). *The Rehabilitation Environment*. Toronto: Lexington Books.
60. Truscott B. (1984). Assessing physiotherapy effectiveness. *Aust. clin. Rev*; Sept: 21–4.

## FURTHER READING

Moos R. H. (1974). *Evaluating Treatment Environments. A Social Ecological Approach*. New York: John Wiley.
Sommer R. (1969). *Personal Space*. New Jersey: Prentice-Hall.

# PART II

# The Motor Relearning Programme

# 1

# *Introduction*

The MRP is made up of seven sections representing the essential functions (motor tasks) of everyday life, most of which are grouped together for ease of reference: upper limb function, oro-facial function, motor tasks performed in sitting and standing, standing up and sitting down, and walking. Sitting up from supine is included as a guide to helping the patient attain an erect posture early after his stroke when he has little motor control.

Within each section is a prescribed plan of action, laid out in four steps (see Table 1.1) and preceded by a description of the normal activity, including the most essential movement components.

The order in which the sections appear is unimportant as there is no intent of progression from section to section. The therapist may start a treatment session with whatever section or part of a section is most appropriate for the patient. Each treatment session will usually, however, comprise material from all sections.

The MRP can be commenced as soon as the patient is medically stable. Should he be confined to bed for a short period following his stroke, he should start on the parts of the Programme which he can manage, for example oro-facial function, upper limb function and extension of the hip in preparation for standing.

The MRP is intended to be sufficient in itself as a programme for the regaining of control over motor tasks. In other words, functional training is in itself remedial. However, other methods of activating muscles and training tasks, which provide auditory or visual evidence of muscle contraction (particularly biofeedback[1,2]) and which assist the patient to contract a previously flaccid muscle or turn off an overactive muscle, may be used in conjunction with the Programme.

Information from research into motor behaviour will no doubt enable the methods of training motor control to become more specific than they are at present. As an example, recent studies of brain function have demonstrated the complex interactions between the two cerebral hemispheres.[3] Whereas the right hemisphere was once considered the 'minor' hemisphere and there was a simplistic view of dominance which implied that one hemisphere was totally dominant, it is now understood that each hemisphere has specialised functions and that the two work together to

29

complement each other. The term 'dominance' is now used to relate to a particular function. For example, the right hemisphere is considered to be dominant in terms of visuospatial functioning, and the left hemisphere in terms of language. An understanding of the functions in which each hemisphere is dominant and of the way in which the hemispheres interact and complement each other in the organisation of behaviour may eventually enable the therapist to determine, in training motor control, those methods of training upon which she should concentrate with a particular patient. Certainly, in administering this Programme, the therapist should consider switching from verbal instruction to visual demonstration or *vice versa* if a person does not, fairly soon, get the idea of the task.

The various sections of the Programme make up the patient's daily therapy sessions, which should range from at least half an hour twice daily in the first few days to daily one-hour sessions or preferably more. However, for learning to take place, tasks the patient has been practising with the therapist will need to be practised outside therapy sessions, and relatives and staff should be encouraged to participate and be trained to give consistent feedback and any assistance necessary. A particular routine or 'drill', carried over from therapy sessions into the rest of the patient's day, is essential for consistency of performance and the learning of motor control.

The plan of action is outlined in four steps (Table 1.1). **Step 1** involves analysis of the patient's performance or his attempts to perform a motor task and any problems associated with its performance. This enables decisions to be made about intervention and enables the goal to be clarified for the patient.

The therapist **observes** the patient and **compares** his performance with the list of essential components. She uses this list as a model of the task and as a framework for analysis, knowing that any alteration in angular displacement of one joint has to be compensated for by a change at another joint. The therapist observes whether or not the patient achieves the goal and analyses the means by which the goal is achieved, **notes** any missing components or incorrect timing of components within the synergy, the absence of muscle activity, the presence of any excessive or inappropriate muscle activity and compensatory motor behaviour.

In analysing standing, for example, she **asks herself questions** about the patient's behaviour. For example, why does his knee hyperextend when he takes weight through it? Is this problem due to lack of control of the quadriceps in 0–15° of extension (neural level)? Is this lack of control associated with unnecessary muscle activity, such as hyperactivity of the plantarflexors? Is his knee position due to abnormal hip alignment (i.e. flexed instead of extended) or due to his knee being pushed back into extension passively by the therapist as she helps him stand up (kinematic level—see Fig. 6.9)? Is his knee position caused by shortened calf muscles (muscular level)? She must differentiate between primary problems and those which are secondary (compensatory) in order to make the correct decision about the problems towards which treatment must be directed.

**Table 1.1** *The four steps in the Motor Relearning Programme*

| | |
|---|---|
| **Step 1** | **Analysis of task** |
| | Observation |
| | Comparison |
| | Analysis |
| **Step 2** | **Practice of missing components** |
| | Explanation—identification of goal |
| | Instruction |
| | Practice + verbal and visual feedback + manual guidance |
| **Step 3** | **Practice of task** |
| | Explanation—identification of goal |
| | Instruction |
| | Practice + verbal and visual feedback + manual guidance |
| | Re-evaluation |
| | Encourage flexibility |
| **Step 4** | **Transference of training** |
| | Opportunity to practise in context |
| | Consistency of practice |
| | Organisation of self-monitored practice |
| | Structured learning environment |
| | Involvement of relatives and staff |

Thus, it is only by making a thorough analysis of each task and its associated problems, which includes any anatomical, biomechanical, physiological and behavioural factors, that the therapist will be able to make the correct decisions about intervention. Examples of the influence of these factors are given throughout the text. The patient is encouraged to contribute to the analysis of his performance to see whether or not he can detect the movement problem himself. If he is encouraged to participate in this way, he will understand what he is to practise and achieve.

In Step 1 for each section there is a guide to analysis of that task with a list of the most commonly missing components and the ways in which a patient may compensate. Having decided on the movement components (and therefore muscle activity) which are poorly controlled or sequenced, it is these components upon which the therapist and patient will concentrate as he practises each particular task. However, if a patient can barely move his hand, it is obvious that he has little muscle activity and is missing many movement components. The therapist will select the muscle activity or components most essential to hand use on which to concentrate in treatment. These, once the patient regains some control over them, will act as triggers to the other components which are synergists for particular activities, as they are the components most likely to generalise into similar tasks.

The assumption underlying the analysis described above is that observation of motor behaviour gives more information about problems of control than the traditional neurological assessment which consists of tests of tone, muscle strength, reflexes and sensation usually performed with the patient in supine and quite unrelated to motor performance. Furthermore, even if the patient can extend his hip and knee against resistance in supine, it does not mean that he will be able to activate these muscles appropriately for tasks such as walking or standing up.

The process of analysis continues throughout **Steps 2 and 3** of the Programme, as the therapist is continually analysing and re-evaluating the patient's performance and the reasons for success or failure, in order to make decisions about the next step in treatment or the next instruction to give. Quick and continuous analysis and decision-making are inter-woven throughout the therapy session and dictate the action taken.

This continuous re-evaluation also provides feedback to the therapist about the effectiveness of analysis and decision-making as well as of treat-ment. If the patient's performance does not improve, the therapist needs to check her original analysis of his problems as well as consider whether or not training was appropriate. Errors in analysis are frequently the cause of ineffective training. Evaluation is, of course, closely linked to expec-tation. For the therapist to see the need for an immediate re-evaluation of her analysis of a particular problem she must have an expectation of success, that is, she must start the treatment session expecting the patient to show some improvement in everything he practises throughout the session.

Although Steps 2 and 3 are separated in order to clarify the part–whole nature of practice, they do in fact overlap, and Step 2 only precedes Step 3 when a patient cannot contract or control the necessary muscles and needs to spend some time practising this component before incorporating it into the complex task.

There are three important points to be considered in using this Programme.

1. **Motor tasks are practised in their entirety.** However, if necess-ary, individual components are practised separately, practice of each com-ponent being followed immediately by practice of the entire activity. Many patients in the early stages will be unable to practise the entire activity, and will have to practise separate movement components, with emphasis thus on the activation of individual muscle groups. The patient must understand what he is practising and this practice must be immedi-ately followed by performance of at least part of the activity for which he is preparing. For example, he may practise activating and controlling his quadriceps in sitting (p. 136), in preparation for controlling flexion–extension of the knee through the mid-stance phase of walking. He will then stand up and practise weight-bearing through the leg and taking a step forward with the intact leg. By practising in this way he will be

able to see where the muscle activity or component fits into the sequence of the entire activity.

'**Components**' in the MRP were originally considered as observable displacements of joints, and the 'essential components' listed for each motor task are actually these displacements. These essential components serve therefore as a baseline for comparison of the patient's performance with so-called normal performance. However, analysis must go beyond this level and take into account other parameters. A 'component' then can become a muscle group (e.g. quadriceps) or a spatio-temporal relationship between muscles in a particular synergy (e.g. the production of appropriate force in the correct temporal sequence of muscles involved in the swing phase of walking).

In some cases, practice of the entire activity with manual guidance from the therapist to ensure normal speed, rhythm, timing and sequencing will actually trigger off the motor activity required, even if at first the patient makes some errors. The negative effect of the errors may be unimportant compared with the positive effect of the rhythm of the activity. Once the patient has the 'idea' of the movement, he can go back to practise particular components in order to become more skilled.

2. **Techniques** principally are those associated with teaching, and comprise methods of identifying the goal and instructions on how to achieve it, verbal and visual feedback and manual guidance. An **explanation** and a **demonstration** will help the patient understand the reason he is having difficulty performing a task, that is, the necessity of the component on which he will concentrate in practice.

**Instructions** are given in the Programme as a guide to the points which should be emphasised to the patient. They should be brief and succinct. These instructions may need to be replaced or reinforced by non-verbal communication, such as gestures and demonstrations, if the patient is dysphasic. Instructions help identify the goal, and some goals seem to facilitate action more readily than others. For example, a patient may not be able to reach forward if the goal is expressed as 'Reach forward', but will do so if the goal is 'Touch the glass'. **Verbal feedback** about his performance, also brief, relevant and concise, may be given at the end of each performance.

**Manual guidance**[4,5] as used in this Programme could be divided into two types. One involves **passive movement** of the patient by the therapist in order to place a limb in a position which enables movement to take place, or to give the patient the idea of the movement (i.e. to present a model of the task). The therapist may move a limb into a specific position so the patient does not have to struggle with what is too difficult (see Fig. 2.12, p. 53), or take the patient through the entire movement once or twice so he gets an idea of his goal and the spatio-temporal characteristics of the task.

The second type of manual guidance involves **spatial and temporal constraint** (or physical restriction) exercised by the therapist over the patient's attempts at a specific motor task. For example, the therapist may hold part of a limb stable to constrain the action spatially while the patient generates a component(s) himself (see Fig. 6.6, p. 104). This cuts down the degrees of freedom which need to be controlled by the patient, allowing him to concentrate on a particular problem of muscle activation associated with achieving the goal. As he develops some control, the therapist decreases her physical constraint so the number of degrees of freedom the patient needs to control is increased. At this point in training, manual guidance can be replaced by verbal guidance and by object-mediated guidance.

Newell[6] considers that manual guidance of this second type in the initial stage of learning shows some benefits to the learner in that it reduces the likelihood of the learner making errors and thus developing bad habits. He raises the question, however, that the benefits of the instructor exercising control of the learner's errors might vary according to the kind of error made by the learner. Where the practice of fundamentally inappropriate actions may hinder learning and create bad habits, errors of execution (i.e. errors in the spatio-temporal details of an action) may be beneficial to skill learning.

This has considerable implications for stroke patients as learners. Therapist-guided active movements, other than for the purposes outlined above, should be avoided as they probably eliminate the learner's need to select the appropriate muscle activity for the required task and the appropriate control mechanism. The therapist should appreciate the effect of her hands on the patient in forcing temporal and spatial details on his performance and in preventing him from seeing the results of his motor activity. It has been found with non-brain-damaged subjects that motivation is low when they cannot make mistakes during practice.[7] It is also evident in normal subjects that with a limb held firmly and guided through a task, there is a tendency for the guidance to turn into a passive movement and for the subject to turn his mind to other matters. In addition, laboratory studies on active and passive movements[8] suggest that information derived from passive movement is different from that derived from active movement.

**Points to check** have been suggested in Steps 2 and 3 in order to indicate errors which are commonly made by the therapist and compensatory strategies commonly used by the patient. The commonest error is failure to monitor body alignment. This monitoring is essential thoughout the therapy session as normal alignment will enable the critical kinematic and kinetic changes to take place and ensure that the appropriate muscles are placed at a mechanical advantage for the action required.

3. **Methods of progression.** It is important that the patient practises at peak performance, his abilities continually being progressed to their limits. Furthermore, he should not waste time by practising what he can already do with ease. Activities are progressed as soon as he has some control. Movements are made more complex by a decrease in manual guidance and feedback, by alterations in speed, and by adding variety. As the patient regains some skill in an activity, he should be exposed to different environmental conditions in order to improve his performance and to enable him to develop the flexibility required for performance in an open environment. During Step 3, as he develops skill, the patient makes the transition from the cognitive phase of learning to the automatic phase of learning.

Many of the methods of progression commonly described in the literature on therapy for stroke[9–11] do not relate to progression in terms of learning but to progression from one piece of apparatus to another which provides less support. Degree of support is therefore the factor by which progress is judged. This ignores the fact that the patient, having learned to walk with a walking frame, then has to learn a different task—to walk with a four-point cane. The latter task involves learning a different set of kinematic and kinetic relationships which are different again from those involved in unaided walking. The assumption has been that if the patient can learn one task he can learn the next. This, however, may not be so. The problem is that the system adapts to the additional support provided[12] by an aid, and the patient will find it difficult to manage without such support and the feedback it engenders. Other no longer tenable methods of progression include ensuring that the patient can roll over before he practises balancing in sitting, can crawl before he can walk, can sit on the floor before he can sit on a stool, can move his shoulder before he can move his hand. The implicit assumption about dyscontrol is that the adult brain-damaged person regresses to the state of motor immaturity seen in infancy, and hence should be trained to perform motor acts in a so-called neurodevelopmental sequence. The assumption here is that acquisition of skill takes place in a certain functional order and that recovery can only take place if this particular order of tasks is practised. However, recent theories and research findings point to a different view both of the nature of dyscontrol and of recovery processes. This enables us to develop new models of therapy based on the theoretical assumptions of this decade and hence to plan more up-to-date means of assisting patients to progress their level of skill.

**Step 4** describes some ways of ensuring that what the patient has been practising in therapy sessions can be practised during the rest of the day. If the patient has been really involved in working out solutions to his problems with his therapist, he will start to apply the same strategies when he is practising on his own. Step 4 is critical because, although the patient may be able to perform a particular component or activity correctly with the therapist, for him to **learn** this component or activity he will need to practise at other times during the day. As well as having the opportunity to practise physically, he should also spend time practising mentally. Ways of organising practice are suggested in each section.

## SPASTICITY

Spasticity seems to be a major concern of the clinician and much emphasis is placed on it in therapy. However, it has been the authors' experience since embarking on a motor learning based approach to therapy that spasticity as described in the literature[13] need not be the major deterrent to the regaining of controlled motor behaviour in most stroke patients. Those patients who do not do very well in therapy have, instead, problems of sustaining muscle activity, of linking muscles together synergically for the performance of motor tasks, of timing the activity of muscles within specific functional synergies, and, in some cases, a total inability to activate muscles for any effective use of the upper limb.

Although spasticity can be characterised by hyperreflexia, hypertonia and clonus, the anatomical and physiological bases for it are still not clearly defined.[14] It has been proposed, however, that when spasticity is slow to develop, the hyperreflexia may be partly due to plastic changes in synaptic connectivity.[14] There have been both anecdotal[15] and experimental[16] reports which indicate that spasticity can be prevented or diminished by certain procedures following brain lesion. It is the present authors' view that a training strategy which involves two factors—(1) the patient working actively to regain motor control, and (2) the prevention of soft tissue contracture—will prevent the slow development of spasticity in most stroke patients.

What is usually called spasticity can be, in many patients following stroke, directly correlated with contracture. This view is shared by others.[17–19] Perry[18] comments that while there are 'no controlled studies documenting that contracture correction reduces spasticity, there are several experiences to support this concept'. Certainly it appears, early following stroke, that it is those muscles which are held persistently in a shortened position which not only develop contracture but which also appear 'easier' for the patient to activate. Such muscles will even contract spontaneously during a cough. The problem is, that as the patient tries to hasten recovery by practising whatever 'movement' he can (often encouraged by the therapist), such activation increases both in force and time, unrelated to specific tasks or goals and unaccompanied therefore by activity in the lengthened muscle groups. In the stroke patient such activity appears to become habitual, certain muscle groups, apparently those whose mechanical advantages are greatest (because of their shortened length), contracting persistently to the disadvantage of others. Gossman, Sahrmann and associates,[20] in their review of length-associated changes in muscle, suggest that the changes in passive tension of the shortened muscle through shortening of connective tissue elements contribute to the clinically perceived 'strength' of these shortened muscles.

If a patient presents with contracture and severe muscle imbalance, the overall objectives of training do not change, although specific attention will need to be paid to overcoming the contractures. An example may make this point clear.

**Example.** A patient some time after a stroke cannot extend his hip in standing and his knee is hyperextended. He cannot overcome this problem, which requires him to 'turn down' the activity in his knee extensors and ankle plantarflexors. The method described on p. 116 for training hip extension will, with a change in some details, achieve this objective. Initially, however, the patient's attention may have to be more on eliminating knee extension and ankle plantarflexion than on contracting the hip extensors. The flexed knee position (with the knee at a right-angle) will make it possible for the patient to activate the knee extensors and ankle dorsiflexors without extending the knee. The therapist pushes down through his knee to discourage ankle plantarflexion while the patient concentrates on pushing his heel down on the floor. He then stands up and practises controlling his hip in extension, stepping forward with the intact leg to ensure weight-bearing through the affected leg with the hip in correct alignment. Such training will only be effective if calf muscle contracture is minimal. In other cases, **serial plasters** will need to be applied for two or three weeks, with training continued during this period. It must be realised that the patient will need to be strongly motivated if he is to change his motor behaviour since this will be difficult and will involve a great deal of practice.

## A NOTE ON SENSORY PROBLEMS

Somatosensory and perceptual-motor problems seem to be relatively common immediately following stroke, but with many people they probably, in these early stages, represent a 'confused' state of mind rather than a real deficit. The patient's sensory dysfunction does not arise from problems of a peripheral nature but from difficulty perceiving and integrating sensory information. The authors' experience with the MRP indicates that the emphasis placed on learning to move and be aware of the affected side and the space it occupies usually corrects these problems and apparently prevents them from becoming established. This may be due to the brain gaining practical experience of monitoring motor performance in conjunction with the therapist's verbal monitoring. Active movement itself provides the sensory information necessary for perception, as action and perception are interdependent.[21][23]

Sensory and perceptual problems should not be considered a poor prognostic sign, as a barrier to rehabilitation, or as a reason for failure in rehabilitation, but as factors to be considered in the design of the patient's entire programme. The physiotherapist and psychologist must work actively in training the patient to overcome these deficits just as the physiotherapist will train the patient to overcome his motor deficit.

Much of the literature on sensory and perceptual problems is confusing. Many studies[24-28] concerned with the relationship between sensory dysfunction and prediction of outcome do not indicate whether or not the patients are having any specific training for their deficits. The results of such studies are frequently conflicting. Some authors suggest that proprioceptive dysfunction, for example, affects outcome, others that this is only when it is combined with dysphasia. Other authors consider it does not affect outcome but may affect length of stay. It is difficult to compare these results because of differences in the methods of measuring outcome.

Some of the confusion in terms of perceptual problems arises because they are little understood, are difficult to describe, to categorise and therefore to test. Roy,[29] for example, has pointed out that although many types of apraxia have been described, little is understood about its true nature. Unfortunately, many neuropsychological tests are multifactorial and in many cases the exact nature of the function which is being tested is unknown.[30,31] Furthermore, the patient may improve his performance of the test but may not improve in any functional activity. In addition, there are few normative data on the sensory and motor abilities of the age group which makes up the largest number of stroke patients.[32,33] It needs to be kept in mind that no matter what tests are devised, the results of assessment are only clinically useful if viewed in terms of providing strategies for remediation.

As has been proposed earlier, many patients immediately following stroke demonstrate what could be called perceptual 'confusion'. For example, they may have some disorder of body image and unilateral spatial neglect. It is as if the person has difficulty organising the material derived from sensory stimuli. He may have a tendency to give up instead of trying to solve the problem or he may make an inappropriate excuse for his difficulty. The MRP, with its emphasis on early weight-bearing through the affected side, training of movement in upright positions, elimination of both unnecessary muscle activity and excessive or unnecessary sensory input to the intact side, patient participation and the use of visual and auditory feedback, appears to prevent the entrenchment of perceptual problems in many patients. Problems may persist, however, in some patients, and a particular deficit will need to be analysed and remediated.

A patient with a perceptual problem is often easily distractable. He may have difficulty shutting out or ignoring extraneous stimuli, noise or bright colours, for example. In this case, he will concentrate better in a quiet room without distractions. Sensory bombardment (by brushing, icing, vibration or towelling), which is sometimes suggested as a means of improving the patient's awareness of his affected side, may increase his confusion, giving him a variety of inputs when he is unable to cope with all the information he is already receiving. Furthermore, McMahon[34] suggests that where vibration is given as part of a generalised sensory regime to increase awareness and responsiveness, it may actually minimise or even prevent the awareness of all subsequent inputs. This illustrates the inappropriateness of arbitrary, non-specific sensory stimulation programmes.

**Astereognosis** and poor **two-point discrimination**, if they persist, will interfere in particular with hand function and may need to be improved by direct practice.[35–37]

If **tactile or visual inattention** (extinction) is present, all stimuli to the intact side should be reduced and stimuli given only to the affected side, with cognitive awareness of the stimulus encouraged. Gradually, the patient is taught to cope with conflicting stimuli to both sides of the body without extinguishing the stimulus to the affected side.

Patients with **visual field defects**, such as homonymous hemianopia, may need to be trained to turn the head to compensate for lack of vision, but it may be possible to train vision within the area of deficit.

**Unilateral spatial neglect**, which may be a persistent problem in some patients, is considered to be accompanied by a shift to one side of the subjective midpoint of the body.[38] Hence the patient tends, visually and physically, to drift towards one side. In therapy, he is made aware of the problem and given a solution. He is constantly reminded of how to regain his body alignment by consciously shifting his weight on to his affected leg and of the need to stay there. A limb load monitor* will help him by providing an auditory reminder of the position of his centre of gravity. He is helped to learn again where the real midline of his body is by using weight-bearing through the affected leg as one anchor and vision as another. Weight-bearing through the affected leg is encouraged if he wears a calico splint (p. 117) to support his knee.

It is worth noting that the patient who drifts to one side does badly if he is held up by the therapist, or is pushed or pulled towards the affected side. The therapist should therefore give only the minimum amount of physical support and guidance. His vision is directed towards his affected side. He is encouraged to search for a particular object. The therapist should also get eye contact and 'draw' his attention towards his affected side by getting him to maintain eye contact as he moves his head. When the patient turns and looks to his affected side, the therapist gives positive reinforcement and reward for his improved behaviour.

From the onset of rehabilitation, the therapist must be careful not to reinforce neglect. If the patient persists, for example, in looking always to one side, the therapist will have to avoid consciously a natural tendency to fit in with this behaviour. She must constantly draw his attention and his gaze towards the affected side by speaking to him from this side, by encouraging weight-bearing through this leg and by instructing other staff in the need to be consistent in this matter. Standing up by pivoting on the intact leg will reinforce a unilateral neglect and will encourage him not to use the affected side (see Fig. 6.13).

Specific training may be necessary for some patients. Weinberg and Diller and their co-workers[39] describe a study in which an experimental group of patients with unilateral spatial neglect was given specific training in visual scanning. In a later study,[40] another experimental group of patients was given training in sensory awareness and spatial reorganisation. Both studies indicated that these patients showed superior performance in the retest compared to the control group which was having 'traditional' rehabilitation. Diller[41] and his colleagues are at present continuing with a study of the effect of a spatial awareness programme upon people with spatial neglect.

**Vision** can be said to have two objectives in respect to movement: the location and appreciation of objects in space, and orientation of the body in space,[42] both of which enable accurate goal-directed motor actions. Visual input thus affects motoneuron excitability in the muscles which are responsible for the movement.[42,43]

A person who is having difficulty with head and trunk control in the sitting position in the first few days following stroke may actually be having difficulty coordinating somatosensory and visual inputs. If he finds it difficult to look at the therapist's face or at his own hand when attempting arm movement, he may be having difficulty locating what he must look at. Normally, when a person needs to locate visually an

*Krusen Research Center, Philadelphia, Pennsylvania.

object within the peripheral visual field, there need to be saccadic eye movements and head movements which enable the object to be imaged by the fovea, which is the most sensitive part of the retina. The central nervous system needs to process the information it receives in order to produce coordination between eye and head movements. The therapist needs to consider the relationship between eye movement, head movement and postural adjustment, for example, by giving the patient practice in searching for (i.e. locating) and fixating on particular objects.

Many stroke patients would normally wear glasses to correct visual dysfunction, particularly when using their hands for fine motor skills, and the therapist should ensure that such a person wears his glasses during therapy.[44] It also needs to be remembered that older people may have decreased visual acuity because of cataract, glaucoma or senile macular degeneration.

Therapists should question existing ways of looking at sensory and perceptual problems and work with psychologists to explore new ideas of remediation. Isaacs[45] reports a suggestion by W. M. R. McLean, for example, that neglect of the left half of space may be due to overactivity of the intact hemisphere, that is, to suppression of the affected side by visual input from the normal side. The suggested treatment, which is under further study, is to obscure the right visual field with special spectacles.

Readers should refer to the appendices and the references throughout the book in order to increase their knowledge of those factors upon which the Programme is based.

## REFERENCES

1. Brudny J., Korein J., Grynbaum B. and Sachs-Frankel G. (1977). Sensory feedback therapy in patients with brain insult. *Scand. J. Rehab. Med*; **9**:155–63.
2. Gonella C., Kolish R. and Hole G. (1978). A commentary on electromyographic feedback in physical therapy. *Phys. Ther*; **58**:11–14.
3. Stockmeyer S. (1980). Hemispheric Specialisation—General Aspects of Importance to Therapists. Unpublished paper given at the *First Austral-Asian Physiotherapy Congress, Singapore*.
4. Holding D. H. (1965). *Principles of Training*. London: Pergamon.
5. Holding D. H. (1970). Learning without errors. In *Psychology of Motor Learning*. (Smith L. E., ed.), pp. 59–81. Chicago: Athletic Institute.
6. Newell K.M. (1981). Skill learning. In *Human Skills* (Holding D. H., ed.), pp. 203–26. New York: John Wiley & Sons.
7. Johnson P. (1984). The acquisition of skill. In *The Psychology of Human Movement* (Smyth M. M. and Wing A. M., eds.), pp. 215–40. New York: Academic Press.
8. Kelso J. A. S. and Wallace S. A. (1978). Conscious mechanisms in movement. In *Information Processing in Motor Control and Learning* (Stelmach G. E., ed.), pp. 79–116. New York: Academic Press.
9. Rehabilitation Study Group (1972). 11 Stroke Rehabilitation. *Stroke*; **3**:381.

10. Licht S. (1975). Stroke rehabilitation program. In *Stroke and its Rehabilitation* (Licht S. ed.) pp. 206–220. New Haven: ELizabeth Licht.

11. Johnstone M. (1983). In *Restoration of Motor Function in the Stroke Patient*, 2nd edn. pp. 17, 149. London: Churchill Livingstone.

12. Brandt T., Krafczyk S. and Malsbender I. (1981). Postural imbalance with head extension: improvement by training as a model for ataxia therapy. *Ann. N. Y. Acad. Sci*, 636–49.

13. Twitchell T. E. (1951). The restoration of motor function following hemiplegia in man. *Brain*; **74**:443.

14. Chapman C. E. and Wiesendanger M. (1982). The physiological and anatomical basis of spasticity: a review. *Physiother. Can*; **34**:125–36.

15. Bobath K. (1980). *A Neurophysiological Basis for the Treatment of Cerebral Palsy*. London: Heinemann Medical.

16. Travis A. M. and Woolsey C. N. (1955). Motor performance of monkeys after bilateral partial and total cerebral decortication. *Brain*; **78**:273.

17. Perry J., Giovan P., Harris L. J., Montgomery J. and Azaria M. (1978). The determinants of muscle action in the hemiparetic lower extremity. *Clin. Orthopaed. & Related Res*; **131**:71–89.

18. Perry J. (1980). Rehabilitation of spasticity. In *Spasticity: Disordered Motor Control*. (Feldman R. G., Young R. R. and Werner K. P., eds.), pp. 87–99. Chicago: Year Book.

19. Herman R. (1970). The myotatic reflex—clinico-physiological aspects of spasticity and contracture. *Brain*; **93**:273–312.

20. Gossman M. R., Sahrmann S. A. and Rose S. J. (1982). Review of length-associated changes in muscle. Experimental evidence and clinical implications. *Phys. Ther*; **62**:1799–808.

21. Neisser U. (1976). *Cognition and Reality*. San Francisco: Freeman.

22. Smyth M. M. (1984). Perception and action. In *The Psychology of Human Movement* (Smyth M. M., Wing A M., eds.), pp. 119 52. London: Academic Press.

23. Fitch H. L., Tuller B. and Turvey M. T. (1982). The Bernstein perspective: III. Tuning of coordinative structures with special reference to perception. In *Human Motor Behavior* (Kelso J. A. S., ed.), pp. 271–82. Hillsdale, New Jersey: Erlbaum.

24. Feigenson J. S., McDowell F. H., Meese P., McCarthy M. L. and Greenberg S. D. (1977). Factors influencing outcome and length of stay in a stroke rehabilitation unit. Part 1. *Stroke*; **8**:651–6.

25. Hurwitz L. J. and Adams G. F. (1972). Rehabilitation of hemiplegia: indices of assessment and prognosis. *Brit. med. J*; 8 January: 94–8.

26. Isaacs B. and Mark R. (1973). Determinants of outcome of stroke rehabilitation. *Age and Ageing*; **2**:139–49.

27. Feigenson J. S., McCarthy M. L., Greenberg S. D. and Feigenson W. D. (1977). Factors influencing outcome and length of stay in a stroke rehabilitation unit. Part 2. *Stroke;* **8**:657–62.

28. McClatchie G. (1980). Survey of rehabilitation outcome of strokes. *Med. J. Aust*; June 28: 649–51.

29. Roy E. A. (1978). Apraxia: a new look at an old syndrome. *J. Human Movt. Studies*; **4**:191–210.

30. Walsh K. (1978). *Neuropsychology and Clinical Approach*. London: Churchill Livingstone.

31. Siev E. and Freishtat B. (1976). *Perceptual Dysfunction in the Adult Stroke Patient*. New Jersey: Charles B. Slack.

32. Welford A. T. (1959). Psychomotor performance. In *Handbook of Aging and*

*the Individual* (Birren J. E. ed.) pp. 562–614. Chicago: University of Chicago Press.

33. Woodburn L. S. (1967). Partial analysis of the neural elements in posture and locomotion. *Psychol. Bull*; **68**:121–48.

34. McMahon C. (1981). Rationale for the use of vibration in the management of tactile defensive patients. *Aust. J. Physiother*; **27**:75–9.

35. Carr J. and Shepherd R. (1980). *Physiotherapy in Disorders of the Brain.* London: Heinemann Medical.

36. Abercrombie M. L. J. (1968). Some notes on spatial disability: movement, intelligence quotient and attentiveness. *Develop. Med. Child Neurol*; **10**:206–13.

37. Inglis J., Sproule M., Leicht M., Donald M. W. and Campbell D. (1976). Electromyographic biofeedback treatment of residual neuromuscular disabilities after cerebrovascular accident. *Physiotherapy Canada*; **28**:260–64.

38. Apfeldorf M. (1962). Perceptual and conceptual processes in case of left-sided spatial inattention. *Percept. Motor Skills*; **14**:419–23.

39. Weinberg J., Diller L., Gordon W., Gerstman L. J., Lieberman A., Lakin P., Hodges G. and Ezrachi O. (1977). Visual scanning training effect on reading-related tasks in acquired right brain damage. *Arch. phys. Med*; **58**:479–86.

40. Weinberg J., Diller L., Gordon W., Gerstman L. J., Lieberman A., Lakin P., Hodges G. and Ezrachi O. (1979). Training sensory awareness and spatial organisation in people with right brain damage. *Arch. phys. Med*; **60**:491–6.

41. Diller L. (1981). Personal communication.

42. Herman R., Herman R. and Maulucci R. (1981). Visually triggered eye-arm movements in man. *Exp. Brain Res*; **42**:392–8.

43. Herman R., Cook T., Cozzins B. and Freedman W. (1974). Control of postural reactions in man: the initiation of gait. In *Control of Posture and Locomotion* (Stein R. B., Pearson K. G., Smith R. S. and Redford J. B. eds.) pp. 363–88. New York: Plenum Press.

44. Macfarlane A. and Longhurst E. C. (1979–80). Visual assessment of cerebrovascular accident patients in rehabilitation programmes. *Australian Orthoptic Journal*; **17**:42–7.

45. Isaacs B. (1977). Stroke research and the physiotherapist. *Physiotherapy*; **63**:366–8.

# 2
# *Upper limb function*

### DESCRIPTION OF NORMAL FUNCTION

Most daily activities involve complex movements of the upper limbs. Motor tasks performed by the upper limb thus illustrate very well the two fundamental problems in motor control raised originally by Bernstein,[1] the problem of degrees of freedom and the problem of context-specific or context-conditioned variability. In daily life the goal of arm movement is often the placement of the hand, for example in pointing, in reaching, or in transporting a grasped object.[2] One needs to be able to:

- grasp and release different objects, of different shapes, sizes, weights, textures

- grasp and release different objects with the arm in different relationships to the body (i.e. close to the body, away from the body)

- transport an object from one place to another (Fig. 2.1)

- move an object about within the hand

- manipulate tools for specific purposes

- reach in all directions (in front, behind, above the head, etc.)

- use two hands together, for example one hand holding and the other moving (Fig. 2.2), both hands doing the same movement (rolling out pastry), both hands doing different movements (piano playing).

These movements are complex because they involve the need to control

**Fig. 2.1** *Note that the posture of the hand in frame 1 is already appropriate for grasping the glass.*

43

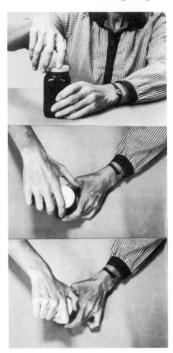

Fig. 2.2 *Putting the lid on a jar. Note the changing relationship between the hands in frames 2 and 3.*

the many joints and muscles that make up a biokinematic multi-linked chain such as the arm (and of course the rest of the body to which the arm is linked). Furthermore, these many degrees of freedom (joints, muscles, motor units) are utilised in different ways according to the **context** in which the person is functioning. As Fig. 2.3 demonstrates, the muscle activity in such a relatively simple movement as lowering the arm depends upon the limb's relationship to gravity and the speed at which it moves.[3] That is, it depends on the purpose or goal of the task and the environment in which the task is performed (its context).

In a general sense, the movement is *shaped* by the requirements of the task. More specifically, the hand itself is shaped by the object it holds. For example, the shape of the glass in Fig. 2.1 and the level of fluid in it determine the grasp, and these plus the location of one's mouth determine how the hand moves through space, the amount of rotation of shoulder and forearm, etc. The hand moulds to the object because of the nature of the object and its use. The muscle activation required to hold the glass throughout its transport to the lips is different in some respects from that required, if, instead of a glass, one were holding a polystyrene cup which would change shape if held too firmly.

There are certain prerequisites for effective use of the upper limb. These are (i) the ability to see what one is doing, (ii) the ability to make the postural adjustments which occur with arm movement and which free the hands for manipulation, and (iii) sensory information.

Information of major importance to motor control comes from certain theories about vision. Gibson[4] wrote of what he called *affordances*, by which he meant the properties of the environment to which we are attuned. When we ask a person to look at what he is doing, we are expecting him to pick up information about an object and the environment that will assist him in carrying out the intended motor task. Tactile information derives from feeling the object in the hand, recognising its nature (that is, its size, shape, form in three dimensions, composition and texture)

Fig. 2.3 *The role of muscles is context dependent.* **L.** *A muscle's action changes according to its angle of pull.* **R.** *A movement is performed by different muscles under different conditions. (From Turvey et al. 1982,[3] with permission.)*

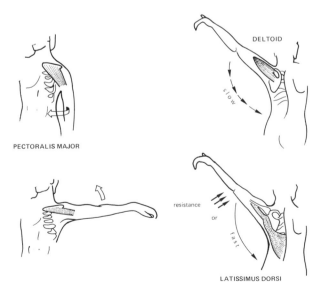

and its position in the hand. Proprioceptive information involves awareness of the relationship of parts of the hand to each other and their position in space. An important aspect of sensory discrimination involves the appreciation of the compressibility of an object, which can be said to involve a combination of dynamaesthesia (the appreciation of the force applied in a motor act), kinaesthesia (the appreciation of change in position of fingers) and the appreciation of counter-pressure of the fingertips.[5]

## ESSENTIAL COMPONENTS

Despite the complexity of upper limb function, it is possible to identify essential movement components, i.e. those components which, when activated, will allow the performance of many different activities. Such muscle–joint components are therefore considered here to be critical parts of many functional synergies involved in everyday motor tasks. Of course, performance of these components alone will not enable complex motor tasks to be performed. These components will need first to be activated by the patient, then combined with other muscle–joint components in particular synergies required for specific tasks.

### Arm

The major function of the arm is to enable the hand to be positioned in space for manipulation (Fig. 2.4). Hence the essential components involved in reaching are:

- shoulder abduction
- shoulder forward flexion
- shoulder extension
- elbow flexion and extension.

**Fig. 2.4** *This subject illustrates the arm and body movements involved in reaching down to pick up a cup.*

These components are always accompanied by appropriate shoulder girdle movements and rotation at the gleno-humeral joint. It should be noted that the ratio of gleno-humeral to scapulo-thoracic movement is 5:4 after the arm has reached 30° of abduction. Before 30° the ratio is approximately 6:1.

## Hand

The major function of the hand is to grasp, release and manipulate objects for specific purposes. Hence the essential components are:

- radial deviation combined with wrist extension (Fig. 2.5)

- wrist extension and flexion while holding an object

- palmar abduction and rotation (opposition) at the carpo-metacarpal joint of the thumb (Fig. 2.6)

- flexion and conjunct rotation (opposition) of individual fingers towards the thumb (Fig. 2.7)

- flexion and extension of the metacarpo-phalangeal joints of the fingers with interphalangeal joints in some flexion

- supination and pronation of the forearm while holding an object.

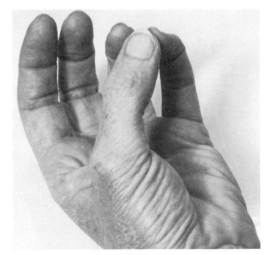

Fig. 2.5

**Fig. 2.5** *Radial deviation, wrist extension and finger flexion are essential components ensuring the optimum posturing of the hand for grasp of different objects for different purposes.*

**Fig. 2.6** *Combined palmar abduction and rotation at the carpo-metacarpal joint is an essential component for optimum posturing of the thumb for manipulation.*

**Fig. 2.7** *The 'cupping' posture of the hand, illustrated here, as the subject touches the thumb to little finger, results from flexion of the finger with conjunct rotation towards the thumb.*

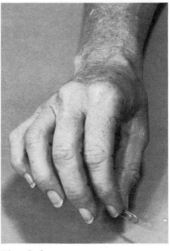

Fig. 2.6

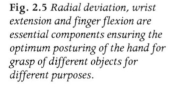

Fig. 2.7

## STEP 1    ANALYSIS OF UPPER LIMB FUNCTION

Immediately following stroke, many patients have no easily observable motor activity in the upper limb. However, even in an apparently flaccid arm, recovering motor activity *can* be found if the therapist understands muscle function well enough to be able to **search actively** for and **detect** small amounts of muscle activity as soon as they occur. In other words, a muscle which may appear non-functioning may contract if the conditions are right. The therapist may enable the patient to elicit muscle activity, for example by altering the goal or by changing the length at which the muscle must contract. What seems certain is that the therapist must set up the necessary conditions for muscle activation. The use of EMG to monitor activity and give feedback to both patient and therapist is probably essential in the early stages.

Analysis of muscle activity around the shoulder can be made with the patient in **supine** (see Fig. 2.12) until he can control his shoulder in sitting without excessive compensatory movements. Muscle activity in the hand is analysed in a similar way but with the **patient sitting at a table.**

Specific problems which may be evident include absence of the essential components plus certain errors of function which illustrate lack of control of the relationship of components within a specific synergy, with some muscles demonstrating depressed activity and others excessive or unnecessary activity.

### Common Problems and Compensatory Strategies

### Arm

- Poor scapular movement (particularly lateral rotation and protraction) and persistent depression of the shoulder girdle.

- Poor muscular control of gleno-humeral joint, that is, lack of shoulder abduction and foward flexion, or inability to sustain these positions. The patient may compensate by using excessive shoulder girdle elevation and lateral flexion of the trunk (Fig. 2.8).

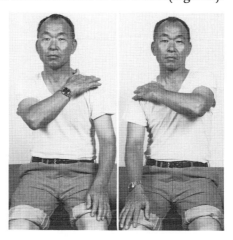

Fig. 2.8 *Excessive left-sided shoulder girdle elevation in frame 2 indicates a poorly controlled relationship between shoulder girdle elevators and shoulder flexors. The patient is compensating for poor control of shoulder flexor muscles. Frame 1 demonstrates normal function of his intact R. arm.*

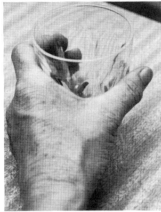

● Excessive and unnecessary elbow flexion, internal rotation of shoulder and pronation of forearm.

### Hand

● Difficulty grasping with wrist in extension. In the absence of wrist extensor activity, the long finger flexors act to flex the wrist as well as the fingers.

● Difficulty extending and flexing the metacarpo-phalangeal joints with the interphalangeal joints in some flexion in order to position the fingers for grasping and releasing an object.

● Difficulty with abduction and rotation of the thumb for grasp and release (Fig. 2.9).

● Inability to release an object without flexing the wrist (Fig. 2.10a).

● Excessive extension of fingers and thumb on release (usually with some wrist flexion).

● Tendency to pronate the forearm excessively while holding on to or picking up an object (Fig. 2.10b).

● Inability to hold different objects while moving the arm.

● Difficulty cupping the hand (Fig. 2.11).

In addition, there are five common sequelae of stroke, all of which are probably preventable.

● Habitual posturing of the limb leading to length-associated changes in the soft tissues of the shoulder, wrist, thumb and fingers.

● Compensation with the intact arm.

● Use of the intact arm to move the affected arm.

● Learned non-use of the affected arm.

**Fig. 2.9 Above.** *Normal posture of hand for grasping a glass.* **Below.** *Note the lack of wrist and MCP joint (of index finger) extension; the lack of abduction at CMC joint and the compensatory abduction and flexion at MCP joint of thumb. The problem in abducting the thumb is due to contracture of web space between thumb and index finger as well as difficulty contracting abductor pollicis brevis in its inner range.*

**Fig. 2.10a** *This man lacks control of his wrist and finger muscles and his long finger flexors have shortened. He lets go of the jar by flexing his wrist, which allows him to pull his hand away.*

**Fig. 2.10b** *Note the posture of the hand on the L. compared to that on the R. The forearm is pronated, the 4th and 5th fingers cannot therefore grasp the glass, and the wrist falls into flexion.*

(a)

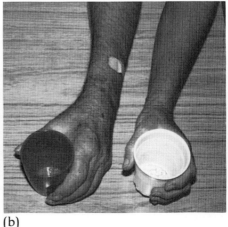

(b)

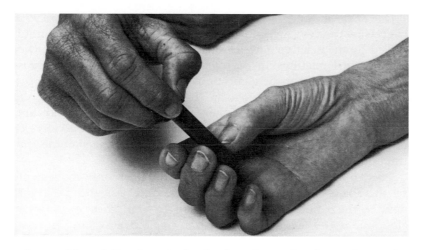

**Fig. 2.11** *Notice the flatness of the ulnar side of the hand as this woman attempts to grasp between thumb and little finger. Compare with Fig. 2.7.*

A major problem following stroke is that the patient's needs can be met by single limb use because these needs are relatively simple. The full impact of functioning with one limb is often only realised once the patient goes home.

## Analysis of the Painful Shoulder

It must be understood that, as a result of depressed motor activity around the shoulder, the surrounding musculature, which normally controls and protects the anatomical relationship of the gleno-humeral joint, is inactive. The gleno humeral joint is not a stable joint, even when the muscles controlling it are functional; when they are inactive, its instability is total.

Soft tissue injury with resultant pain, stiffness and subluxation will usually result from four mechanical factors: (a) pinching of soft tissue against the acromion, (b) friction of soft tissue against bone, (c) traction to soft tissue, and (d) soft tissue contracture. The first three factors may be brought about by the following: passive range of motion exercises; exercises which tend to force abduction without external rotation; exercises which involve movement from a position of internal rotation and flexion, into elevation and abduction, then into external rotation and extension; the effect of gravity plus the weight of the flaccid arm; pulling on the limb to position the patient; rolling on to the paretic shoulder. In addition to these factors, there is very often a failure in therapy to use the appropriate means of eliciting muscular activity and of training motor control around the shoulder.

The pathological conditions which develop include degeneration of the acromio-clavicular joint, bicipital tendinitis, bursitis, coracoiditis, and supraspinatus tendinitis.[6] Several authors[6,7] describe the occurrence of brachial plexus lesion following stroke, caused by traction on the unprotected shoulder and resulting in true muscle paralysis which may take 8 to 12 months or more to recover, if it recovers at all.

The mechanism of the painful shoulder is discussed in some detail by Najenson and his colleagues,[8] Cailliet,[6] and Griffin and Reddin.[9]

One of the major causes of a painful, stiff shoulder is the use of **passive exercises.** Passive range of motion exercises, because they cannot be controlled by the inactive muscles surrounding the joint, may allow or force an abnormal relationship between humerus and scapula because they involve movement at the gleno-humeral joint without the corresponding and necessary movement of the shoulder girdle. They will therefore damage the soft tissues around the gleno-humeral joint. In addition, many stroke patients are elderly, and with increasing age degenerative changes develop within the rotator cuff[10] and predispose the shoulder to injury through passive movement.

Passive range of motion exercises include not only movements done by therapists or nurses, but also pulley exercises and passive ranging done by the patient himself using his intact arm. These exercises are usually done with the objective of preventing stiffness and soft tissue contracture. However, the patient will not develop a stiff shoulder if damage to the soft tissues is avoided and if, early following stroke, the therapist trains muscle activity with the arm in elevation (see Fig. 2.12).

Any complaint of pain from a patient should be analysed to establish a cause so that the necessary therapy can be commenced. Unfortunately, the therapist may react to pain and stiffness in the hemiplegic patient by stepping up passive movements in the belief that inactivity is causing the pain. This causes further trauma and increases the symptoms. These problems of musculo-skeletal origin should be diagnosed and analysed, and the therapy which would normally be given to a patient with such problems should be instituted as soon as possible. For example, if **pain** is the problem, treatment may include peripheral joint mobilisation,[11] interferential or transcutaneous nerve stimulation. If **chronic inflammation** exists, heat or ultrasound may stimulate a more normal repair process. There are two possible components of **joint stiffness**: (i) adaptive tissue contracture secondary to disuse, and (ii) adhesions between normally free-sliding structures. The former will improve if the patient practises the movement outlined in this Programme, within a gradually increasing pain-free range. The latter will respond to peripheral joint mobilisation in addition to the practice of appropriate movements.

### STEPS 2 AND 3    PRACTICE OF UPPER LIMB FUNCTION

In general, the literature suggests that rehabilitation of upper limb function is unsuccessful, a large proportion of patients never re-establishing effective use of the arm and many of them developing a painful shoulder[6–8,12–20] for a variety of different reasons. It is probable that this is an unnecessary state of affairs and is due to some extent to inappropriate treatment techniques and a tendency to 'wait' for obvious signs of recovery before giving any active therapy.[18]

Motor activity can usually be elicited early with the patient in supine with his arm in elevation (see Fig. 2.12). Frequently, muscles can be activated initially in an eccentric rather than concentric mode, and at a particular length. It is difficult for the patient to activate muscles around the shoulder with his arm by his side, either in sitting or lying, as the muscles required to lift the limb are at a mechanical disadvantage.

Another important factor to consider is the way in which muscles normally function. Individual muscles or parts of muscles function with other muscles in a variety of synergies, depending upon the task being performed. Therefore, following stroke, a muscle may be activated as part of one particular synergy before it can be activated as part of another. Similarly, if a muscle cannot contract for its prime mover function, it may be able to contract as a synergist.

The first part of this section is relevant for the patient who, early after his stroke, apparently has little or no motor activity in the upper limb. The objective is to discover what motor activity exists by giving particular muscles the opportunity to contract as they normally would for a particular task, to point out to the patient what he can do and to encourage and help him to extend his abilities. The therapist and nurse do not need to do passive range of motion exercises to maintain joint range, as the activities outlined below will have the effect of lengthening muscles held in habitually shortened positions.

The following points should be kept in mind throughout this part of the Programme.

- Arm movements, including movements of the hand, must be trained early following stroke. Hand movements must not be left until there is some recovery of function around the shoulder, as suggested by some authors.[21] Recovery does **not** necessarily take place from proximal to distal, as is sometimes suggested, nor is it necessary to have control of the shoulder before attempting to regain control of the hand.

- Motor tasks involving upper limb function are made up of very complex combinations of muscle action. As soon as isolated muscle action is elicited, this must be practised and extended into meaningful tasks, with the patient gaining control over increasing ranges of a movement, changing to other movements which also require the muscle to contract in its prime mover, synergist and fixator roles, shifting from concentric to eccentric in different parts of range and at various speeds.

- All muscle activity unnecessary to the movement being attempted must be eliminated consciously by the patient. This includes movements of the intact side of the body (including the 'fidgeting' seen in some patients) and muscular activity in the affected arm which is not necessary for the particular movement or activity being practised. Elimination of unnecessary muscle activity is part of the development of motor control and, in the case of unnecessary activity of the affected arm, appears to minimise the development of the flexor overactivity seen in some patients.

- Gross therapist-controlled patterns of movements of the upper limb should be avoided as these will not allow either the therapist or the patient to be aware of any minimal muscle activity present and they will tend to encourage only the more active muscles (usually those which tend to become shortened) to contract, and they may cause trauma around the shoulder (for example bicipital tendinitis).[6]

● Activity should be elicited at first in the position of greatest advantage to the muscle. For example, in supine, arm flexed at 90° for the deltoid muscle.

● It is important that the therapist does not hold the limb too firmly since this may actually prevent the patient from activating muscles by removing the need to do so. In addition, the limb should not be supported once sufficient muscle activity has been retrained. The manual guidance required when there is insufficient muscle activity is changed to verbal guidance as soon as possible.

● If a muscle does not contract in a particular set of conditions, vary the conditions. For example, change the speed of movement, the relationship to gravity, or the goal.

● Muscles must not be encouraged to contract incorrectly. That is, exercises should not be given which stimulate muscles to contract concentrically throughout an entire range of movement when this is unnatural in terms of the limb's changing relationship to gravity. An example of the latter is the change in muscle activity involved when the arm is moved from the side to above the head in the supine position.

● The goal should be clearly identified and should be of such a nature that the patient will know whether or not he has achieved it. Similarly, the patient should not be encouraged to practise movements which have no functional significance. For example, he should not be given a rubber ball to squeeze as this encourages habituation of flexor activity, is usually combined with wrist flexion and pronation and therefore aids the development of a fixed flexion posture.

● Should stereotyped muscle overactivity and muscle shortening interfere with the training of arm movements and this cannot be overcome by conscious control, the cycle of overactivity and misplaced effort will need to be overcome by other means. Application of serial plasters, combined with practice of reaching and pointing, will often enable a patient to acquire some control over upper limb tasks which may otherwise be impossible. EMG feedback may also enable a patient who is prepared to persevere to get the idea of how to turn down (or off) unwanted muscle activity.

● The therapist should not think in terms of strengthening muscles in a general sense. The objective is to help the patient elicit muscle activity and to train him to control this activity for specific tasks (in specific contexts). As he practises various tasks, he will acquire the appropriate muscular strength and endurance relatively easily, provided he is given the opportunity to work to the point of mild muscular fatigue. He should increase the number of repetitions of certain tasks daily and the task should be modified so his strength increases for similar tasks. For example, a pointing task can be modified to a task involving lifting increasingly heavier objects above the head.

● Tasks involving both arms should be introduced as soon as possible. In certain tasks (see Fig. 2.2) the two limbs seem to function as part of the one synergy which includes the object(s) being manipulated, and, because of the apparently context-specific nature of control processes, these tasks will need to be specifically practised to be relearned.

● Although it is useful to perform a particular movement passively in order to give the patient the idea of the movement (to clarify the goal), persistence with passive movement may prevent him from eliciting any muscular activity by interfering with his attempts. In addition, passive movements make it difficult for the therapist to recognise any muscle activity which may occur and to feed back to the patient this information which is essential to the learning process. Passive movements probably play little part in promoting motor learning since the information derived from passive movement is different from that derived from active movement. The limb may, of course, need to be passively positioned by the therapist (see Fig. 2.12).

## To Elicit Muscle Activity and Train Motor Control for Reaching and Pointing

*Supine, therapist lifts the patient's arm and supports it in forward flexion. Patient attempts to reach up towards ceiling (Fig. 2.12).*

NOTE
This may also be done in side lying.

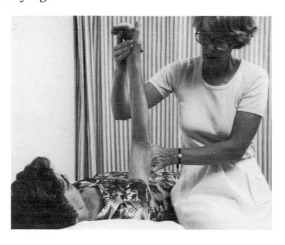

**Fig. 2.12** *This woman is practising reaching upwards. The therapist has assisted the arm into the flexed position and is holding it to prevent it from internally rotating. She reminds the patient to keep her elbow straight.*

INSTRUCTIONS
'Reach up towards the ceiling.'
'Think about using your shoulder.'
'Now let your shoulder go back on to the bed.'

CHECK
Ensure scapula moves—it may have to be moved passively into position during the first few attempts.
Do not allow forearm to pronate or gleno-humeral joint to internally rotate.
Do not allow the patient to retract the shoulder actively—the return movement should involve eccentric muscle activity.

*Supine, therapist lifts patient's arm and supports it in forward flexion. She helps the patient elicit muscle activity by asking him to attempt parts of various tasks, for example: (i) to take his hand to his head (Fig. 2.13); (ii) to take his hand above his head to the pillow (Fig. 2.14). This is an exploratory procedure, the patient trying to elicit muscle activity in certain key muscles (Fig. 2.15), particularly in deltoid and triceps brachii.*

NOTE
While only minimal muscle activity is present around the shoulder, the patient may complain of pain in the shoulder when the arm is passively raised to 90°. This may be due to nipping of soft tissues between the humeral head and acromion. It is usually relieved if the therapist separates the joint surfaces **minimally**. This is discontinued as soon as it is no longer necessary.

(i) INSTRUCTIONS
'See if you can take your hand down to your forehead—gently—don't let your hand drop. Now lift it up a little.'

CHECK
Do not allow patient to pronate forearm.
The palm should go to the forehead.

**Fig. 2.13** *This woman is able to control an eccentric contraction of her triceps in inner range. Beyond this the therapist took some of the weight of the arm. The therapist supports the gleno-humeral joint.*

**Fig. 2.14** *This woman is stretching her hand above her head with the therapist's guidance. From this position she can also practise lifting her hand off the pillow, i.e. extending her elbow.*

Fig. 2.13

Fig. 2.14

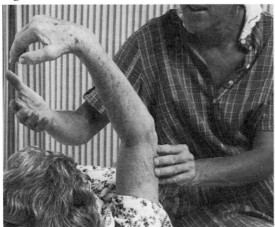

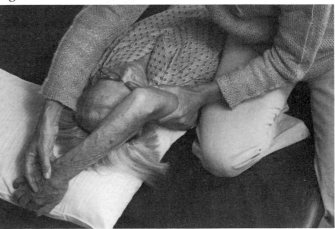

(ii) INSTRUCTIONS

'See if you can take your hand above your head to the pillow. I'll help you.'

'Keep your arm in near your head.'

'Now try to reach above your head.'

CHECK

Do not allow patient to pronate forearm.

Do not allow shoulder to abduct.

Check that scapula movement takes place.

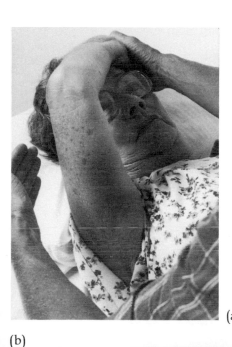

(a)

Fig. 2.15 (a) *The therapist holds this woman's hand on her head while she practises lowering her elbow to the pillow.* (b) *In this photograph, she is lifting her arm, moving her hand to her head, then her arm back to the therapist's leg.* (c) *She has difficulty controlling supination and needs to practise this separately. This practice is followed by taking her hand to her head again.*

(b)

(c)

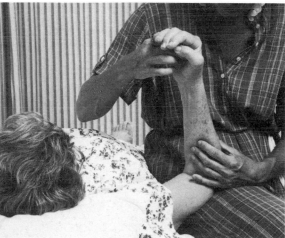

As soon as the patient has some control over such muscles as deltoid, pectorals and triceps, he should progress to the following activities.

*Patient practises holding his arm in forward flexion and moving it within an ever-increasing range, in all directions, always maintaining control (Fig. 2.16). Therapist indicates the required trajectory.*

INSTRUCTIONS
'Stretch up with your hand—keep your elbow straight.'
'See if you can follow my hand.'

CHECK
Do not allow forearm to pronate, elbow to flex, or shoulder to internally rotate excessively.

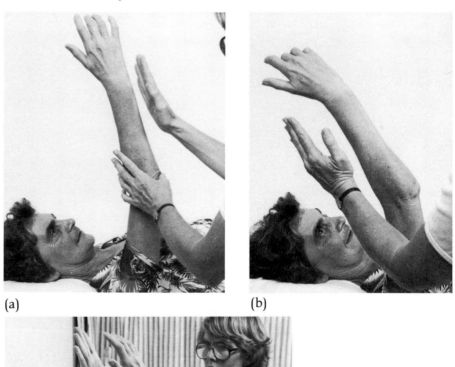

(a)                                                        (b)

(c)

**Fig. 2.16** *This woman is improving control over reaching. In* **(a)** *she needs some assistance to keep her arm from abducting. In* **(b)** *she needs only guidance as she follows the directional cue given by the therapist. Part of her practice involves switching from a concentric contraction of her shoulder flexor muscles to an eccentric contraction of her extensors as the movement changes direction. In* **(c)** *she shows how she can now control abduction and adduction of her arm in forward flexion.*

Followed by:

*Sitting at a table, patient practises reaching forward and upward (Fig. 2.17a). He should work within the range he can control, gradually increasing it. When he can control his shoulder above 90°, he practises reaching below 90° in small but increasing ranges of movement, until he can reach from a position with his arm by his side, both in flexion and in abduction, and in sitting as well as in standing.*

INSTRUCTIONS
'Reach out to touch this. Don't let your arm drop.'

CHECK
Do not allow elevation of the shoulder girdle as a substitute for abduction or flexion of the shoulder.
Do not allow elbow to flex unless it is required by the position of the object.
Make sure patient reaches forward with shoulder externally rotating. There is a tendency to reach with the shoulder in internal rotation (Fig. 2.17b and c).

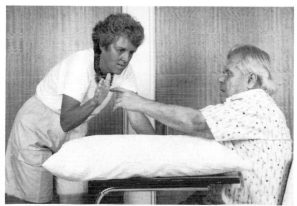

(a)

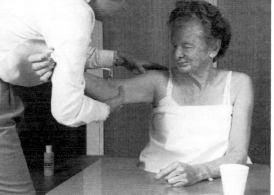

(b)                              (c)

**Fig. 2.17a** *This man is practising reaching and pointing. The therapist ensures that the path through which the hand and elbow pass is appropriate. He is reminded not to elevate his shoulder girdle.*

**Fig. 2.17b** *This woman reaches for the cup with her shoulder internally rotating and shoulder girdle elevated. In (c) the therapist is helping her to practise reaching forward with her shoulder externally rotating. Note the improved alignment of her shoulder girdle.*

## To Maintain Length of Muscles

*The patient sits with his hands or just his affected hand flat on the bed behind him. The therapist will need to assist him (Fig. 2.18).*

NOTE
This helps prevent contracture of the long finger flexors, shoulder flexors and internal rotators.

CHECK
Make sure patient's weight really does go backwards and that he does take weight through the affected hand.
Do not allow elbow to bend.

*With the patient in sitting or standing, therapist helps him to keep his hand on the wall, with the arm abducted/flexed forward at 90°. Therapist helps him place the arm in this position. Some horizontal pressure through the arm will prevent the hand from sliding down the wall. Initially, the therapist may need to hold the elbow extended. In this position, the patient practises bending and straightening the elbow in order to improve control over the elbow extensors and, as he regains some shoulder and elbow control, he practises turning his trunk and head (Fig. 2.19).*

NOTE
It is important to prevent contracture and length-associated changes in wrist and finger flexors as this will cause pain and interfere with training of hand function. The above is also used to train muscle control around the shoulder and elbow.

Fig. 2.18

Fig. 2.19

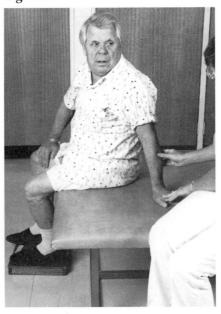

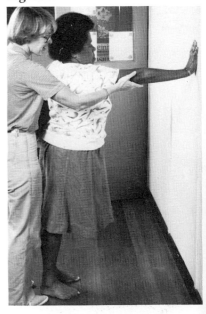

**Fig. 2.18** *The therapist has assisted this man to place his hand flat on the bench and has asked him to lean on to this hand. She sits with him and ensures that the elbow does not bend while they plan the next part of the session.*

**Fig. 2.19** *The therapist helps this woman to keep her hand on the wall while asking her to turn her trunk and head to the left.*

INSTRUCTIONS

'Let your elbow bend a little. Straighten your elbow by pushing the heel of your hand into the wall gently.'

Progress to:

'Keep your hand on the wall and turn your body to face the front/side. Make sure your hand doesn't slip.'

CHECK

Do not allow hand to slide down wall.

Draw his attention to his hand. Make sure weight is on both feet and shoulders are level.

## To Elicit Muscle Activity and Train Motor Control for Manipulation

### To Train Wrist Extension

NOTE

It is usually more effective to elicit wrist extensor activity by practising radial deviation of the wrist (Fig. 2.20a).

*Patient sitting with arm supported on the table, forearm in mid position, fingers and thumb around a glass. He attempts to lift the object up (Fig. 2.20).*

INSTRUCTIONS

'Lift the glass up.'

'Let it down slowly.'

Once the patient has elicited some extensor activity

Progress to:

*With forearm in mid position, patient practises lifting object up, extending wrist, putting it down again, flexing wrist, putting it down again. He should hold the object throughout (Fig. 2.20b).*

INSTRUCTIONS

'Move the jar to this point on the table.'

**Fig. 2.20a** *This man is asked to lift the glass up and to lower it without losing control at his wrist. The therapist holds the forearm in mid position and helps the patient hold the glass so he can concentrate on activating his wrist muscles.*

**Fig. 2.20b** *This man practises lifting an object up from the table and putting it down again, in different ranges of flexion and extension, using radial deviation not elbow flexion.*

(a)

(b)

*The patient can also practise moving his hand back so he touches an object. The distance to be moved can be increased as soon as possible. The goal can be changed so he pushes the object along the table (Fig. 2.21), which involves some arm as well as wrist movement.*

**CHECK**

Correct tendency for wrist to flex when it should be extending. Discourage any tendency for forearm to pronate.

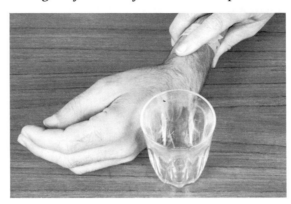

**Fig. 2.21** *This man's goal is to push the glass along the table by extending his wrist with forearm in mid position.*

## To Train Supination

*Fingers around cylindrical object, patient attempts to supinate forearm so end of object touches table (Fig. 2.22).*

**NOTE**

The goal can be changed by having him make an impression on a piece of putty (Fig. 2.23). The task can be changed by having him hold out his hand palm upward to receive small objects such as rice grains.

**Fig. 2.22** *The goal is to touch the table with the top of the bottle. The therapist is helping him practise in the inner range of supination where he has particular difficulty. He should not move his shoulder.*

**Fig. 2.23** *Practice of supinating the forearm. The goal is to make an impression on the putty with his third metacarpal.*

**INSTRUCTIONS**

'Touch the top of the bottle to the table—if you can't hold it firmly enough, I'll help you.'

**CHECK**

Do not allow forearm to lift off table unless required by the task.

Fig. 2.22

Fig. 2.23

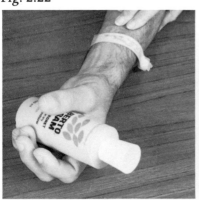

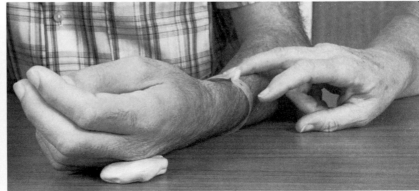

## To Train Palmar Abduction and Rotation of the Thumb
## (Opposition)

*Therapist holds forearm in mid position and wrist in extension while patient attempts to grasp and release a glass (Fig. 2.24). The therapist will need to guide the movement until there is some muscle control (Fig. 2.24a).*

NOTE

The therapist guides the patient's hand towards the object. This action, with its intention to take hold of the object, may encourage the thumb to abduct and the fingers to extend at the metacarpo-phalangeal joints.

INSTRUCTIONS

'Open your hand to take this. I'll help you.'
'Now, let it go.'

CHECK

Do not allow wrist to flex or forearm to pronate.
When he has some thumb movement, make sure he abducts the thumb during release and does not slide it up the object by extending carpo-metacarpal joint (Fig. 2.24b).

Fig. 2.24 (a) *Therapist holds thumb, fingers and wrist in a posture which enables the patient to grasp the object.* (b) *This woman, in releasing the bandage, has extended her thumb instead of abducting it. She needs to practise the component of palmar abduction.* (c) *It is important that in all hand activities the therapist ensures the correct posture of the thumb and fingers. Here, during practice of wrist movement, the patient is holding his thumb incorrectly. It is flexed at the metacarpal joint instead of being abducted in a palmar direction.*

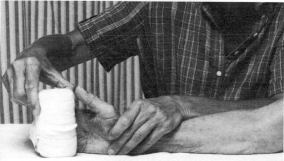

(c)

Make sure the thumb posture is correct, that is, pad of thumb grasps object, not medial border (Fig. 2.24c).

*Patient attempts to push a light object away by abducting the carpo-metacarpal joint.*

NOTE
Another similar task is to move the thumb sideways to touch the object.

INSTRUCTIONS
'See if you can push this away gently with your thumb.'
'See if you can push it a little further—to this line on the table.'

CHECK
Discourage wrist flexion as a compensation for poor thumb abduction.

## To Train Opposition of Radial and Ulnar Sides of Hand (Cupping of the Hand)

*Forearm in supination, patient practises opposing thumb and other fingers, particularly fourth and fifth fingers (Fig. 2.25). Therapist demonstrates how the palm of the hand should cup.*

INSTRUCTIONS
'Touch the tip of your little finger to your thumb. Make sure you move your finger as well as your thumb.'
'Cup your hand.'

CHECK
Make sure movement occurs at carpo-metacarpal joint and not just at metacarpo-phalangeal joint.
Tips of fingers and thumb should touch.

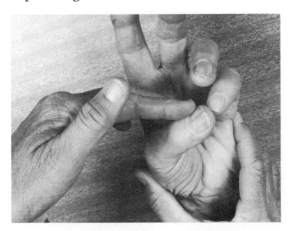

**Fig. 2.25** *Practice of opposition between thumb and little finger. Therapist guides the cupping movement.*

## To Train Manipulation of Objects

Below are some suggestions indicating some of the varied activities the patient should practise.

*Patient practises picking up various small objects between thumb and each finger (Fig. 2.26). He can go on to picking these out of a bowl and releasing them into another bowl, supinating his hand while holding the object, etc.*

INSTRUCTIONS
'Pick this up and put it here.'

CHECK
Make sure patient uses the pad of the thumb for holding object, not the medial side.

Make sure the wrist is not actively flexing while releasing the object (see Fig. 2.10a), although depending on arm position and task, the wrist may need to be held in a flexed position.

**Fig. 2.26** *Therapist needs to assist this patient to control the correct posture of the hand.*

*Patient practises picking up polystyrene cup around the rim without deforming it (Fig. 2.27a). He should practise picking it up, holding it while moving his arm, and releasing it. He should do this with his hand close to his body, away from his body, and in conjunction with the other hand (for example, pouring water from one cup to another, Fig. 2.27b).*

**Fig. 2.27a** *This man is concentrating on controlling his grasp so as not to deform the cup. He should also practise holding the cup at its side. He should be reminded to keep his left shoulder down.*

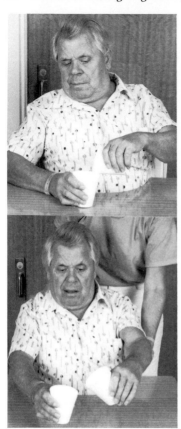

**Fig. 2.27b** *This man is practising a bimanual activity—pouring water from one cup to the other.* **Top.** *He is accomplishing the task but by elevating his shoulder girdle, internally rotating his shoulder and resting one cup on the other.* **Bottom.** *He practises with arms out in front, concentrating on getting the necessary combination of internal rotation and pronation without shoulder girdle elevation. Note the improved alignment of his shoulders and head.*

NOTE
This will train dynamaesthesia as well as motor control.

INSTRUCTIONS
'Pick up this cup—don't change its shape.'

CHECK
Do not allow patient to grip inappropriately, that is, so firmly that he deforms it or so gently that he drops it.

*Patient practises picking a piece of paper from his opposite shoulder (Fig. 2.28).*

CHECK
Point out errors in synergic relationships.

In order to use the hand effectively, it is necessary to have a fine degree of control over the shoulder, elbow and wrist, since this is what enables the hand to reach its goal. The following are some examples of how **to increase complexity.**

- Reaching forward to pick up or touch an object.
- Reaching sideways to pick up an object from a table and transferring it to a table in front.
- Grasping and releasing an object with the arm stretched out behind (see Fig. 5.10).
- Using two hands together to perform various tasks.

CHECK
Correct any tendency to use the incorrect musculature or an inappropriate degree of motor activity, for example excessive elevation of the shoulder girdle as a substitute for forward flexion or abduction of the shoulder.

**Fig. 2.28** *Practice of picking an object off the shoulder.*

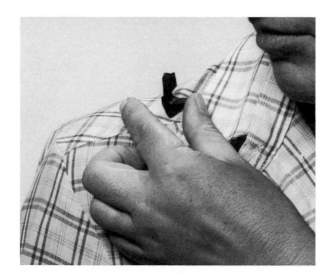

The patient should not keep practising what he can already do, but should keep progressing towards more difficult tasks. If he finds a particular component of a movement difficult or if the therapist sees he is having difficulty controlling or performing a particular movement, he should practise this in as many ways and for as many different tasks as possible. For example, if he is having difficulty supinating to hold his hand out palm upward, he can practise a variety of tasks which require the last few degrees of supination.

When training the affected limb to perform a function which is normally bimanual (for example, in the use of tools such as knife and fork), the patient may use his affected hand more efficiently if he also uses the intact hand for the relevant part of the task.

For the patient to learn to manipulate a particular tool (toothbrush, comb, tools of trade) requires from the therapist a specific analysis of each function to determine the missing components in the synergy. This means that the therapist should know which are the essential components for the use of that tool. Examples of how to train a patient in the use of cutlery are given below.

### To Improve the Use of Cutlery

Throughout practice, the therapist must constantly compare the patient's performance with the normal (Fig. 2.29). Manipulative activities are very complex, yet a patient will often be able to improve his performance quickly if the therapist can pick out the major factor interfering with that performance. Certain problems are particularly common and require specific training.

### The Fork

1. Difficulty moving fork into position in hand once it is picked up.

*With forearm in pronation, patient practises turning small objects over in the palm of his hand using his fingers and thumb.*

Followed by:

*Patient practises picking up fork and moving it into position in his hand.*

2. Difficulty holding fork between thumb, index and middle fingers (Fig. 2.29a).

*Patient practises picking up small objects between thumb, index and middle fingers.*

Followed by:

*Patient uses fork with therapist's guidance.*

CHECK
Do not allow him to pronate forearm excessively.

**Fig. 2.29 (a)** *and* **(c)** *illustrate the method of holding cutlery which is being trained below;* **(b)** *shows the position of the knife and fork in the palm of the hand.*

(a)

(b)

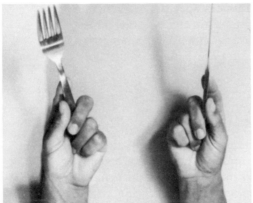

3. Difficulty holding fork between ring and little fingers and palm (Fig. 2.29b).

*Patient practises picking up a jelly bean between thumb and ring finger, thumb and little finger, supinating and pronating the forearm while holding the object, putting it in a bowl.*

CHECK
Make sure he picks up with tips of thumb and fingers. Followed by:

*Patient uses fork with therapist's guidance.*

CHECK
Do not allow him to pronate forearm excessively.

4. Difficulty holding fork while pressing down on food.

*Patient practises using fork to hold food and to pick it up with therapist's guidance.*

CHECK
Do not allow patient to pronate forearm excessively.
Make sure he can make the change from active flexion while pressing down on fork to active extension as he lifts food from the plate or moves fork elsewhere on plate.

NOTE

Whenever the patient practises manipulating his fork, he will do better if he holds a knife in his other hand, and if he has before him a plate with food (for example cheese) on it.

## The Knife

The difficulties listed above are also seen when using a knife and should be trained in a similar manner. Below are some examples of difficulties specifically related to the use of a knife.

1. Difficulty holding knife while cutting meat.

*Patient practises using knife to cut food with therapist's guidance.*

CHECK

Do not allow him to press down too hard.
Do not allow him to pronate forearm excessively.

2. Difficulty pushing food towards fork.

*Patient practises using knife to push food towards fork.*

CHECK

Do not allow him to pronate excessively.

## The Spoon

1. Difficulty moving spoon into position in hand once it is picked up.

*With forearm in supination, patient practises touching thumb and each fingertip separately as quickly as possible while maintaining accuracy.*

*With forearm in supination, patient practises turning over a small object in his hand.*

2. Difficulty adjusting grasp in order to keep bowl of spoon level as it is raised from plate to mouth (Fig. 2.29c).

*Patient practises moving his arm while holding spoon. Spoon should contain fluid, as this will be a useful monitoring device for him.*

Followed by:

*Patient practises taking spoon (with fluid) to mouth.*

CHECK

Do not allow him to take his head down to the spoon.

## STEP 4    TRANSFERENCE OF TRAINING INTO DAILY LIFE

If the patient is to achieve his potential recovery of upper limb function, there are four points which must be considered.

1. He must not suffer **secondary soft tissue injury**. It is possible for the shoulder to be injured by any member of the staff, by a relative and by the patient himself. Nurses, therapists, porters and doctors must not pull on the patient's arm to move him about. Passive movements to check for joint range limitation or with the objective of maintaining or increasing joint range may damage the soft tissues around the paretic shoulder joint. The patient should not be encouraged to move his affected arm passively and he should not be given pulley exercises. Both activities fail to take into account normal scapulo-humeral rhythm and therefore increase the likelihood of soft tissue injury in the shoulder region.

2. He must not be allowed or encouraged to develop **'learned non-use'**[22] of his affected arm, by performing activities which involve movement of the affected limb by the intact limb or by moving about using only the intact limbs. During these activities, the patient will be attending only to the arm which can move and not at all to the affected one. Several studies with de-afferentated and brain-damaged monkeys[22,23] indicate that unrestrained use of the intact limb may be a major factor in failure to recover function in the affected limb. If the animal's intact limb is restrained and he is trained to use the affected limb, he regains effective use of this limb. The possibility of physically restraining the affected limb of a human for short periods of the day has recently been reported,[24] but, as the authors point out, further research is needed. However, therapist, nurse and relatives should discourage, using verbal restraint and explanation, any unnecessary and compensatory activity in the intact limb. The patient should understand the reason for this restraint and should try not to use his intact arm unnecessarily.

3. During the day the patient should **practise** particular components

**Fig. 2.30** *Length-associated muscle changes will quickly develop if the person's arm remains in one position for long periods during the day.*

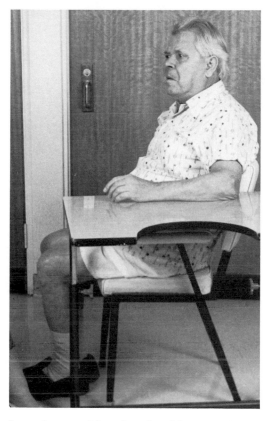

**Fig. 2.31** *Sitting with arm in this position is part of a daily programme to prevent contracture of shoulder muscles.*

or movements on which the therapist considers he should concentrate. Movements which are too difficult to practise on his own can be practised mentally (see p. 176). However, the therapist should, whenever possible, teach a relative or friend how to help the patient practise movements or movement components, and the patient should have a notebook in which details of what he should practise are listed, with photographs if possible.

4. Persistent posturing of the limb is a particular problem (Fig. 2.30) in the early stages following stroke. The flaccid or inactive limb is held by the side in internal rotation and flexion, causing **length-associated changes** to occur, probably quite rapidly,[25] and allowing the glenohumeral joint to sublux downwards. A daily programme of changing the limb posture and daily training sessions involving movements such as those illustrated earlier should prevent marked contractures from occurring, but the risk remains until control of the limb is regained. The tendency for the shoulder joint to sublux may, in addition, be avoided by the wearing of a support (see below) while taking a shower or during prolonged standing. During sitting, the arm should be supported on a table, alternately in forward flexion and abduction (Fig. 2.31). This will help avoid depression of the shoulder girdle which alters the angle of the glenoid cavity and predisposes the shoulder joint to subluxation (Fig. 2.32).

The use of different types of support is questionable.[26-31] Certainly,

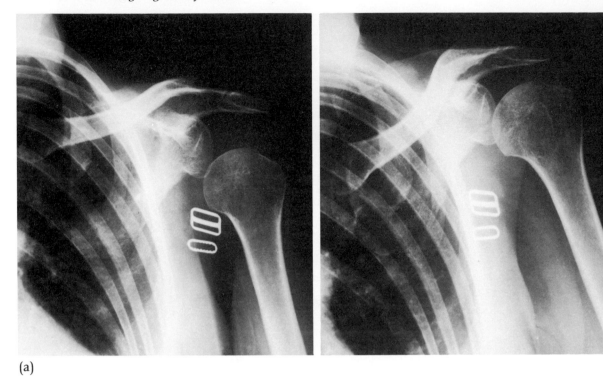

(a)                                                                    (b)

**Fig. 2.32** *Note the difference in the position of the head of the humerus in these two pictures. Radiography of five different slings showed no effect upon the degree of subluxation:* **(a)** *illustrates one of these slings,* **(b)** *illustrates the effect of supporting the same patient's arm on pillows.*

they can be remarkably ineffectual. The authors examined radiologically the effects of five different types of support on a particular patient with subluxation of the shoulder. None of them made any difference at all. Figure 2.32 illustrates the effect of one. There appears to be no support which has been shown by radiographic study to be effective. However, a harness has recently been devised* and is being investigated for effectiveness. It is important that a method is found which protects the paretic shoulder from injury and traction while the patient walks around. There must be a balance between protecting the shoulder from injury, preventing neglect or 'learned non-use' of the limb, and ensuring the best position for the regaining of motor control. A major objective remains the early recovery of motor control around an undamaged shoulder.

The value of hand splints following stroke is a controversial point and Einbond[32] and Neuhaus and colleagues[33] describe the inconsistent and confusing rationale expressed by both the non-splinting group of therapists and the splinting group. This confusion is probably an illustration of the lack of understanding both of the problems of upper limb function following stroke and of the proper objectives of rehabilitation. Furthermore, the pathophysiology of stroke seems to be assumed to be the same as for brain damage following head injury and for cerebral palsy. Hence, the motor problems and their treatment are assumed, probably incorrectly, to be the same.

*Hook hemi-harness. Created by the Orthopedic Equipment Company, Bourbon, Indiana, USA 46504, in conjunction with the August E. Hook Physical Rehabilitation Center.

Unfortunately, much splinting is applied by therapists who have negative expectations of recovery of upper limb function. Hence, such splinting may actually prevent the patient regaining any motor control by preventing use of the hand.

Splinting, if it needs to be considered, must fulfil the objective of enabling muscles to regain function, by putting joints in a position which favours the relearning of certain movement components or motor tasks. If, for example, moulded plastic is used to hold the thumb in a position of some palmar abduction in the early stages before the person has regained control of the thumb, and if this splint is small enough not to interfere with the person's practice of hand movement, then it may well be effective in helping the person to regain control of thumb abduction, grasp and release. Contracture of the thumb web is a common problem and develops very early following stroke.

## REFERENCES

1. Bernstein N. (1967). *The Coordination and Regulation of Movement*. New York: Pergamon.
2. Hollerbach J. M. and Flash T. (1982). Dynamic interactions between limb segments during planar arm movement. *Biol. Cybern*; **44**:67–77.
3. Turvey M. T., Fitch H. L. and Tuller B. (1982). The Bernstein perspective: I. The problems of degrees of freedom and context-conditioned variability. In *Human Motor Behavior* (Kelso J. A. S., ed.), pp. 247. Hillsdale, New Jersey: Erlbaum.
4. Gibson J. J. (1977). The theory of affordances. In *Perceiving, Acting and Knowing* (Shaw R. and Bransford J., eds.), pp. 67–82. Hillsdale, New Jersey: Erlbaum.
5. Roland P. E. (1973). Lack of appreciation of compressibility, adynamaesthesia and akinaesthesia. *J. neurol. Sci*; **20**:51–61.
6. Caillict R. (1980). *The Shoulder in Hemiplegia*. Philadelphia: F. A. Davis.
7. Kaplan P. E., Meredith J., Taft G. and Betts H. B. (1977). Stroke and brachial plexus injury: a difficult problem. *Arch. phys. Med*; **58**, **9**:415–18.
8. Najenson T., Yacubovich E. and Pikielni S. (1971). Rotator cuff injury in shoulder joints of hemiplegic patients. *Scand. J. Rehab. Med*; **3**:131–7.
9. Griffin J. and Reddin G. (1981). Shoulder pain in patients with hemiplegia. *Phys. Therapy* **61**, 7:1041–5.
10. Mosley H. F. (1963). The vascular supply of the rotator cuff. *Surg. Clin. N. Amer*; **43**:1521–2.
11. Maitland G. D. (1977). *Peripheral Manipulation*, 2nd edn. London: Butterworths.
12. Caldwell C. B., Wilson D. J. and Braun R. M. (1969). Evaluation and treatment of the upper extremity in the hemiplegic stroke patient. *Clinical Orthopaedics and Related Research*; **63**:69–93.
13. Moskowitz H., Goodman C. R. and Smith E. (1969). Hemiplegic shoulder. *N.Y. St. J. Med*; **69**:548–50.
14. Loombs J. (1973). Facilitation techniques in hemiplegia: treatment of the arm. *Physiotherapy Canada*; **25**, 5:283–8.
15. Mossman P. L. (1976). *A Problem-Orientated Approach to Stroke Rehabilitation*. Illinois: Charles C. Thomas.
16. Davis S. W., Petrillo C. R., Rodolfo D. E. and Chu D. S. (1977). Shoulder-hand

syndrome in a hemiplegic population: a 5-year retrospective study. *Arch. phys. Med*; **58**: 353–6.

17. Brocklehurst J., Andrews K., Richards B. and Laycock P. J. (1978). How much physical therapy for patients with stroke? *Brit. med J*; 20 May: 1307–10.
18. Johnstone M. (1978). *Restoration of Motor Function in the Stroke Patient*. London: Churchill Livingstone.
19. Jensen E. M. (1980). The hemiplegic shoulder. *Scand. J. Rehab. Med*, Suppl; **7**:113–119.
20. Carr J. and Shepherd R. (1982). The neglected upper limb following stroke. Paper delivered at the First Australasian Physiotherapy Congress, Singapore.
21. Dardier E. (1980). *The Early Stroke Patient*. London: Baillière Tindall.
22. Taub E. (1980). Somato-sensory deafferentation research with monkeys: implications for rehabilitation medicine. In *Behavioral Psychology in Rehabilitation Medicine: Clinical Applications* (Ince L. P., ed.) pp. 371–401 Baltimore: Williams and Wilkins.
23. Yu J. (1976). Functional recovery with and without training following brain damage in experimental animals: a review. *Arch. phys. Med*; **57**:38–41.
24. Ostendorf C. G. and Wolf S. L. (1981). Effect of forced use of the upper extremity of a hemiplegic patient on changes in function. *Phys. Ther*; **61**:1022–28.
25. Gossman M. R., Sahrmann S. A. and Rose S. J. (1982). Review of length-associated changes in muscle. Experimental evidence and clinical implications. *Phys. Ther*; **62**:1799–808.
26. Voss D. (1969). Should patients with hemiplegia wear a sling? *Phys. Ther*; **49**:1030.
27. Braun R. M. (1969). Should patients with hemiplegia wear a sling? *Phys. Ther*; **49**:1029–30.
28. Hurd M. M., Farrell K. H. and Waylonis G. W. (1974). Shoulder sling for hemiplegia: friend or foe? *Arch. phys Med*; **55**:519–22.
29. Bobath B. (1978). *Adult Hemiplegia: Evaluation and Treatment*, 2nd edn. London: Heinemann Medical.
30. Wilson D. and Caldwell C. B. (1978). A treatment approach emphasizing upper extremity orthoses. *Phys. Ther*; **58**:313–20.
31. Neal M. R. and Williamson J. (1980). Collar sling for bilateral shoulder subluxation. *Amer. J. occup. Ther*; **34**:400–401.
32. Einbond A. (1978). *Survey of Occupational Therapists' Criteria for Splinting Hemiplegic Hands: Rational or Ritual?* Paper submitted in partial fulfillment of the requirement for the degree of Master of Science, available from Columbia University, New York.
33. Neuhaus B. E. *et al.* (1981). A survey of rationales for and against hand splinting in hemiplegia. *Amer. J. occup. Ther*; **35**:83–90.

# 3

# *Oro-facial function*

Oro-facial function comprises various activities, such as **swallowing, facial expression, ventilation** and the **motor aspects of speech production.** Following stroke, all these activities may be affected, interfering with eating, communication and socialisation. Oro-facial problems, particularly drooling, are embarrassing and frustrating, have a devastating effect on the patient and his relatives, and influence people's attitudes. The patient's low self-esteem will interfere with him doing his best in therapy and practice sessions. Concentration becomes directed towards looking for a tissue and wiping his mouth. The prospect of dribbling thus becomes a powerful influence on his behaviour. Remediation of these problems should therefore begin immediately, as they respond very quickly to early treatment.

In the first few days, it is the ineffective **swallowing** which causes the greatest dysfunction. The resultant drooling, aspiration and difficulty ingesting food bring about a poor nutritional state and may lead to the provision of a nasogastric tube. It is particularly important that normal swallowing is retrained as soon as possible. The use of a nasogastric tube should be avoided, as nasogastric tube feeding is unpleasant and may cause hypersensitivity of the oral area. It leads to irritation of the mucous membrane, lack of stimulus to chew or move the tongue, and predisposes to oesophageal reflux.[1] As the patient is not taking food normally, he is deprived of the pleasure of eating and drinking as well as of the stimuli provided by different types of food. More normal swallowing will occur once the patient has jaw and lip closure, a more mobile tongue and the stimulus of something to swallow.

## DESCRIPTION OF NORMAL SWALLOWING

Swallowing is a highly complex and integrated neuromuscular function.[2,3] The initial stage, the preparation of the bolus, is under voluntary control, but once the bolus is passed into the oral pharynx the second, or involuntary, stage of the act of swallowing begins. It is the contact of the bolus or saliva with the mucosa of the back of the tongue and pharynx which sets up the swallowing reflex. During the involuntary stage the food passes through the pharynx to the oesophagus, partly under the influence of gravity with the person in the erect position and partly due to the successive contraction of the constrictor muscles.

Food is taken into the mouth with the lips and is bitten by the front teeth. The tongue moves the food on to the molars and mixes the food with salivary secretions. The cheek, comprising the buccinator muscle, also assists in controlling the food in the mouth by pushing the food back on to the molars when the action of chewing tends to push it sideways.

The tongue selects the food that is sufficiently moistened for swallowing. The anterior part of the tongue is raised and pressed against the hard palate just behind the front teeth. The bolus is formed on the tongue and squeezed backwards towards the posterior oral cavity by movement of the tongue against the hard palate. This movement commences at the tip of the tongue and spreads back rapidly.[3] To help form the bolus, the soft palate closes down on to the back of the tongue. The bolus is passed into the oral pharynx through the palatoglossal arches by elevation of the posterior third of the tongue in a postero-superior direction. In swallowing fluids, the intrinsic muscles of the tongue are used to form a tunnel with the hard palate and to squirt fluid back through the mouth.

In preparation for swallowing, the hyoid bone is brought forward into a position of moderate elevation through the movements of the tongue. The lips and jaw are closed and the soft palate and uvula made tense to seal off the nasopharynx. The larynx is pulled upward behind the hyoid bone and towards the back of the tongue. This narrows the lumen of the larynx which helps to protect the respiratory tract. As the bolus reaches the epiglottis, some of it spills sideways descending on one or both sides of the larynx into the oesophagus. The pharynx is also pulled upwards over the bolus, propelling it a short distance into the oesophagus. Once the bolus enters the oesophagus it continues downward by peristaltic action. Breathing is inhibited momentarily during swallowing.

## ESSENTIAL COMPONENTS

- Jaw closure.

- Lip closure.

- Elevation of posterior third of tongue to close off posterior oral cavity.

- Elevation of lateral borders of tongue.

There are certain prerequisites which are necessary for effective swallowing.

- The sitting position.

- Control of breathing in relation to swallowing.

- Normal reflex activity (the gag reflex is the only oral reflex normally present in the adult).

**STEP 1    ANALYSIS OF ORO-FACIAL FUNCTION**

Analysis of oro-facial function involves:

- observation of the alignment and movements of lips, jaws and tongue
- intra-oral digital examination of tongue and cheeks (to test threshold to touch and to establish whether the tongue offers the normal resistance to movement)
- observation of eating and drinking.

### Difficulty with Swallowing

Lack of control over oro-facial musculature, in particular:

- open jaw
- poor lip seal
- immobile tongue (tongue may look enlarged and be too far forward)

will result in:

- drooling
- food collecting between cheek and gums. Although this is often attributed to lack of muscle activity in the cheek (buccinator), a major factor is probably the immobility of the tongue.

Altered threshold to stimulation will result in:

- diminished awareness, which will cause difficulty keeping false teeth in place and a lack of awareness of saliva and food in the mouth, or
- hypersensitivity, which will be demonstrated by a hyperactive gag reflex, retraction of the tongue, and aversion to touch and to the presence of food in the mouth. This occurs as a secondary problem, due to fear of choking in untreated patients and after prolonged use of a nasogastric tube.

### Imbalance of Facial Movements and Expression

This is the result of lack of motor control of the lower part of the face on the affected side, together with overactivity and unopposed activity of the face on the intact side. The upper third of the face receives bilateral innervation and therefore is not usually affected following stroke.

## Lack of Emotional Control

Although not an oro-facial problem *per se*, lack of control over the physical manifestations of the emotions is frequently seen in the early stages following stroke. This lack of control is demonstrated by outbursts of uncontrolled crying which the patient has difficulty modifying or stopping. If the patient is not given a solution to this problem, it is very likely to persist and to interfere with his training programme, with his regaining of self-esteem and with his personal relationships.

## Poor Breathing Control

This may result from a combination of factors including poor control over the soft palate, or motor impersistence,[4,5] which is demonstrated by difficulty in taking a deep breath, holding the breath, and controlling a prolonged expiration, thus making communication difficult.

### STEPS 2 AND 3    PRACTICE OF ORO-FACIAL FUNCTION

The most efficient position for swallowing, and therefore for eating, is sitting. The therapist should check the patient's sitting position and ensure that he is sitting with hips well back in the chair and with his head and trunk erect.

The patient who wears false teeth should be helped to put them in place. This will improve his appearance, reduce his embarrassment and prevent his gums from altering. His improved appearance will have a positive effect on the people around him.

The use of a spatula is not recommended in treatment because of its unpleasant texture and because the therapist's finger is a more effective tool for evaluating oral function.

The lips and intra-oral area are sensitive to temperature change. Ice, which is sometimes used to stimulate oral function, has in fact a numbing effect which increases the patient's difficulty in moving his tongue around his mouth or in knowing if his lips are closed or not. Sucking an ice block may also cause him to aspirate, as liquids are more easily aspirated than solids.[1]

In the intra-oral techniques described below, most of which were devised by Mueller,[6] the therapist should not persist for too long as the presence of the finger in the mouth will interfere with the normal sequence of swallowing. Intra-oral techniques should be interrupted frequently and the jaw held closed in order to allow the patient to swallow. Presence of saliva and closure of the jaw and lips will combine with the improved muscular activity of the tongue to trigger off swallowing.

### To Train Swallowing

## To Train Jaw Closure

*Tongue must be inside mouth. Therapist closes jaw and holds it closed with atlanto-occipital joint in the mid position (Fig. 3.1). This gives the patient the idea of the movement.*

NOTE
The jaw can be held closed momentarily or the patient reminded to keep his jaw closed during therapy sessions whenever necessary, that is, whenever the jaw hangs open and whenever the patient needs to swallow.

INSTRUCTIONS
'Close your mouth and jaw.'
'Keep your teeth gently together.'
'Now open your mouth and close it again.'
'Relax this (intact) side of your mouth.'

CHECK
When assisting, make sure head is not pushed back.
Make sure teeth are occluded.
Make sure mouth opens symmetrically (see Fig. 3.4c).

## To Train Lip Closure

*Therapist holds the jaw closed, using her finger to indicate to the patient the lip area which is not functioning (see Fig. 3.1).*

INSTRUCTIONS
'Keep your lips gently together.'
'Relax this (intact) side of your face.'

CHECK
Do not allow patient to suck on lower lip as this interferes with tongue movement for swallowing.

Do not encourage patient to pout.
Jaw must be closed.
Make sure nose is clear.

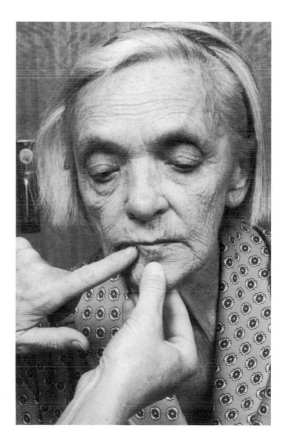

**Fig. 3.1** *Therapist holds the jaw closed and asks this woman to keep her lips gently together.*

## To Train Tongue Movement

*Therapist uses index finger to give horizontal digital vibration to the anterior third of tongue with firm pressure downwards (Fig. 3.2). The amplitude of the vibratory movement should be small and the therapist's finger should not be in the mouth any longer than 5 seconds. The therapist then assists with jaw closure.*

INSTRUCTIONS

'Open your mouth. I'm going to give you the idea of where your tongue should be when you swallow.'
'Now close your mouth.'

CHECK

Tell patient when he has swallowed—he may not know.
When assisting jaw closure, make sure head is not pushed back.
Do not put finger(s) too far back on tongue.
Make sure you push downwards on the tongue.
Do not repeatedly ask the patient to swallow—swallowing in the absence of saliva requires effort.[7]

**Fig. 3.2** *Vibratory stimulation to the tongue in a horizontal direction with firm pressure downwards.*

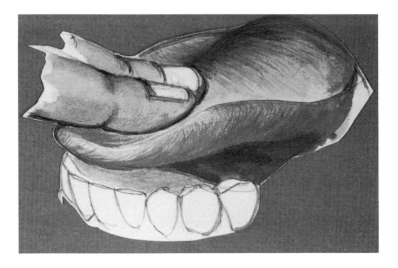

## To Elevate Posterior Third of Tongue

*Therapist uses index finger to give firm pressure to the anterior third of the tongue in a downwards direction to close off posterior oral cavity (Fig. 3.3). Follow immediately with lip and jaw closure as before.*

INSTRUCTIONS

'Open your mouth. I'm going to push down on your tongue to help you to swallow.'
'Now close your mouth.'
'Can you feel the back of your throat close off when you swallow?'

CHECK
As above.

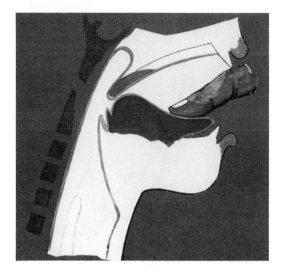

**Fig. 3.3** *Firm pressure downwards elicits elevation of the posterior third of the tongue to close off the posterior oral cavity.*

## Eating and Drinking

Liquid is more easily aspirated than food, hence the patient will gain some confidence in his ability to swallow without choking if he practises swallowing solids before he attempts liquids. Food should be palatable, consist of a variety of textures, and initially should be of the consistency of mashed potatoes. Bosma[2] comments that thickened food is usually handled with relative safety. Pureed food or food which goes sloppy in the mouth will not provide the stimulus needed for regaining normal oral function and may be easily aspirated. The patient should also be given food of different textures as well as chewable food. If he has difficulty with chewing, he may find it easier if the therapist holds his jaw lightly closed.

## To Train Facial Movements

*Patient practises decreasing the overactivity of the intact side of his face while opening and closing his mouth (Fig. 3.4). Therapist indicates with her finger where to relax (Fig. 3.4b) and where to move.*

INSTRUCTIONS
'Open your mouth.'
'Relax this side of your face.'
'Now close it again.'

NOTE
Do not give bilateral facial exercises, as these will increase the tendency towards overactivity of the intact side. Many patients are only able to activate muscles on the affected side once they have decreased the over-activity of the intact side.

**Fig. 3.4** *In* **(a)** *the imbalance of movement can be seen when this man opens his mouth.* **(b)** *The therapist encourages him to 'turn down' the overactivity on the R. side of his face. In* **(c)** *he can now perform the task with better control. (From Carr and Shepherd 1986,[8] with permission.)*

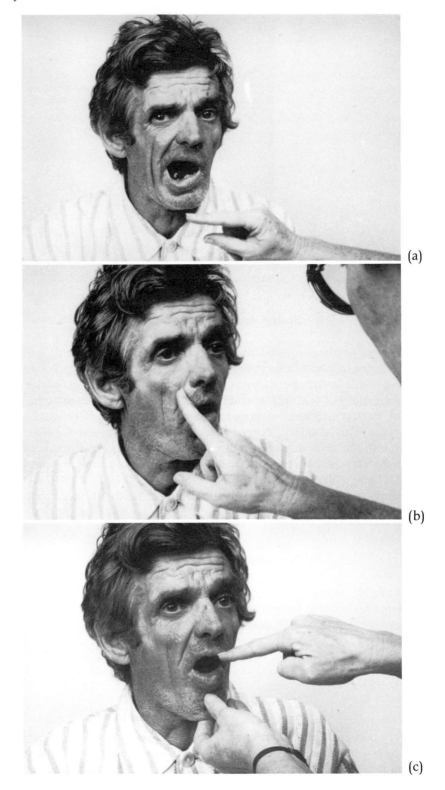

(a)

(b)

(c)

### To Improve Breathing Control

NOTE

Some patients have difficulty with breathing control following stroke, either because respirations are too shallow, or because they cannot be sustained. Shallow respirations leave the patient prone to respiratory infections and do not allow effective oxygenation. Lack of sustained respiration interferes with vocalisation. The following technique is useful in both cases.

*Patient sits with trunk inclined forward, arms resting on a table. He practises deep breathing with the emphasis on expiration. Therapist gives overpressure and vibrations on lower third of rib cage on expiration (Fig. 3.5). This can be combined with the patient making a sound on expiration. The patient can also experiment with varying the sound. This provides useful auditory feedback. This technique is also useful as preparation for speech therapy.*

INSTRUCTIONS

'Take a deep breath. Breathe right out.'
'Make it last as long as you can. I'll count.'
'Now say "ah", "m" as you breathe out.'

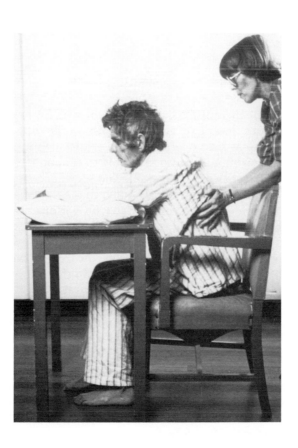

**Fig. 3.5** *Practice of deep breathing and sustaining a sound.*

### To Improve Control over Emotional Outbursts

Assistance overcoming this problem is provided by training to improve control over oral musculature and ventilation and care not to reinforce the problem so the patient learns to modify his behaviour. He should be reassured that the therapist understands the problem and the strategies for overcoming it. The therapist's manner should be calm as she gives him instructions to help him modify his behaviour.

*Whenever the patient looks as if he is about to cry.*

INSTRUCTIONS
'Take a deep breath.'
'Now just breathe quietly through your nose.'

NOTE
The patient will learn to use this strategy when necessary.

*If the patient has lost control and is actually crying, therapist holds jaw closed gently.*

INSTRUCTION
'Take a deep breath and stop crying.'
When patient gains control, 'Good'.

### STEP 4    TRANSFERENCE OF TRAINING INTO DAILY LIFE

The therapist assists the patient with his first few meals, using the techniques described above to train swallowing. This should be done just before at least one meal a day while such intervention is necessary. The patient should sit up at a table to eat and mealtimes should be organised so that they are pleasurable and social occasions.

During all training sessions, the therapist monitors the patient's facial posture while he concentrates on various tasks, indicating to him when his jaw is open and reminding him to keep his mouth closed.

The patient who is having difficulty keeping his false teeth in place because of diminished sensory awareness should be shown how to rub his gums briskly, and he should do this himself prior to putting his teeth in.

The strategy for gaining control over emotional outbursts (described above) can be explained to nursing staff and relatives, so they will be able to reinforce this behaviour when necessary. Consistency in this will prevent emotional outbursts from becoming habitual.

Improved oro-facial control and appearance will help the patient regain self-esteem and confidence in personal interactions with staff, relatives and other people, as well as improve his nutritional state. The oro-facial problems described above are quickly overcome if therapy is instituted within the first few days .

# REFERENCES

1. Larsen G. J. (1972). Rehabilitation for dysphagia paralytica. *J. Speech Dis;* **37**:187–94.
2. Bosma J. F. (1957). Deglutition: pharyngeal stage. *Physiol. Rev;* **37**:275.
3. Williams P. L. and Warwick R., eds (1980). *Gray's Anatomy,* 36th edn. London: Churchill Livingstone.
4. Fisher M. (1956). Left hemiplegia and motor impersistence. *J. nerv. ment. Dis;* **123**:201–18.
5. Ben-Yishay Y., Diller L., Gerstman L. and Haas A. (1968). The relationship between impersistence, intellectual function and outcome of rehabilitation in patients with left hemiplegia. *Neurology;* **18**:852–61.
6. Mueller H. (1971). Personal communication.
7. Kydd W. L. and Toda J. (1962). Tongue pressure exerted on the hard palate during swallowing. *J. Amer. dent. Ass;* **65**:319–30.
8. Carr J. H. and Shepherd R. B. (1986). Motor training following stroke. In *International Perspectives in Physical Therapy* (Banks M., ed.). London: Churchill Livingstone.

# 4

# *Sitting up over the side of the bed*

Most people, when they sit up over the side of the bed, go from supine to sitting up, use the hands for leverage and swing the legs over the side of the bed. The elderly often turn to one side first, use their hands to push themselves up, then swing the legs over the side. In the early stages following stroke, it is practical and more effective for the patient to be assisted to turn on to his intact side and to sit up from this position. There are three reasons for this: (i) it avoids the unrestrained use of the intact arm which results when the patient tries to pull himself up from supine into sitting, (ii) it is a quick and easy way for the patient to sit up with minimal help from another person, and (iii) it gives him the idea of how to do it himself.

At this early stage, learning to move again is concentrated on motor activities in sitting and standing. However, rather than bodily lifting the patient into sitting, the therapist gives him the opportunity to relearn the essential components of the task. He is thus assisted to participate as much as he can in sitting up without undue effort and overuse of the intact side.

If the therapist applies leverage correctly at his shoulder and pelvis and if the patient lifts his own head laterally, sitting up requires very little effort from either therapist or patient. It is recommended that only a minimum period of time be spent on this section, as it is more important that the patient spends his therapy session practising more significant tasks.

## DESCRIPTION OF NORMAL FUNCTION

In turning on to one side, say the right, the head flexes and rotates towards the right, the left arm flexes at the shoulder, the shoulder girdle protracts, the left leg flexes at the hip and knee and the foot pushes into the bed to provide leverage and to roll the body over. The underneath leg is usually flexed at the hip and knee, and the hips are shifted backwards in order to give a more stable base of support.

In order to sit up over the side of the bed from the side-lying position, the neck and trunk flex laterally, the lower arm abducts into the bed to provide leverage and the legs are lifted and swung over the side of the bed (Fig. 4.1).

*Fig. 4.1 Sitting up over the side of the bed. Note the lateral flexion of neck and trunk.*

**NOTE**

Rolling over is often given excessive emphasis in rehabilitation.[1,2] In the early stages, the patient is relatively helpless in supine and it is better for the therapist to assist him on to his side and to concentrate his practice sessions on other activities which are more stimulating as well as being more relevant for a person who should be spending his day out of bed.

## ESSENTIAL COMPONENTS

*Turning on to the side*

- Rotation and flexion of neck.

- Hip and knee flexion.

- Flexion of shoulder and protraction of shoulder girdle.

- Rotation within the trunk.

*Sitting up over side of bed (Fig. 4.1)*

- Lateral flexion of neck.

- Lateral flexion of trunk (abduction of the lower arm occurs as these two components are performed).

- Legs lifted and lowered over side of bed.

## STEP 1   ANALYSIS OF SITTING UP OVER SIDE OF BED

In **turning on to the intact side**, the patient may demonstrate particular difficulty in:

- flexion of hip and knee on affected side

- flexion of shoulder and protraction of shoulder girdle.

These problems will result in:

- inappropriate compensatory movements of the intact side, e.g. he may try to wriggle or to pull himself over using his intact hand.

In addition:

- failure to make an attempt to move the affected arm passively across his body may indicate that he is neglecting the affected side.

In **sitting up over the side of the bed**, the following problems may occur in compensation for the depressed muscle activity.

- Patient rotates neck and flexes it forward instead of flexing it laterally. This usually occurs because of poor lateral trunk movement (Fig. 4.2).
- Patient pulls with intact hand (at bedclothes or side of bed) instead of laterally flexing neck and trunk.
- Patient hooks intact leg under affected leg in order to get legs over side of bed. This will shift his weight back as he attempts to sit up.

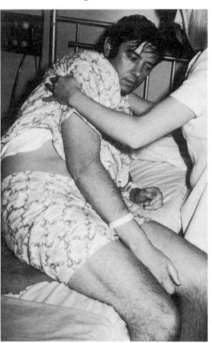

**Fig. 4.2** *This man is having difficulty laterally flexing his head and trunk. Note also that his hips are insufficiently flexed, and that his weight is too far back.*

### STEP 2    PRACTICE OF MISSING COMPONENT

NOTE

Therapist assists patient on to his intact side. It is important that he does not have to struggle. The therapist encourages him to turn his head, assists him to bring his shoulder and arm forward, and to flex his hips and knees (Fig. 4.3). She may have to adjust his pelvis and legs in order to provide a stable base of support once he has turned on to his side.

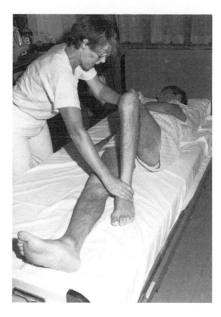

**Fig. 4.3** *The therapist helps this man roll on to his side. She holds his leg steady while he pushes down through his foot to turn his body. If he needs more assistance, she will help him lift his L. shoulder and turn.*

## To Train Lateral Flexion of Neck

*Therapist assists patient to lift his head off the pillow and patient attempts to lower his head to the pillow, contracting his lateral flexors eccentrically. He then practises lifting his head sideways unaided (Fig. 4.4).*

INSTRUCTIONS
'Lower your head to the pillow.'
'Lift your head from the pillow.'
'This is what you will do when I help you sit up over the side of the bed.'

CHECK
Do not allow neck to rotate or flex forward.

**Fig. 4.4** *Practice of lifting the head from the pillow. The therapist takes some of the weight during lifting if necessary.*

**STEP 3    PRACTICE OF SITTING UP FROM SIDE LYING**

### To Assist Patient to Sit over Side of Bed

*Patient lifts his head laterally, while therapist, with one hand under the shoulder and the other pushing downwards on his pelvis, helps him to move up into the sitting position. Therapist may need to assist his legs over the side of the bed (Fig. 4.5).*

INSTRUCTIONS
'Lift your head sideways.'
'Now, sit up and I'll help you.'

CHECK
Do not pull on patient's arm.
Remind him to keep his head moving sideways.
It may be necessary to move his legs over the side of the bed before commencing the movement.
Do not let his weight go backwards.
The patient will use his intact arm for leverage without prompting.

**Fig. 4.5** *Therapist assists this man to sit up.* **(a)** *Movement of the legs over side of bed.* **(b)** *Pressure down on the pelvis provides a fulcrum which enables the patient to be assisted easily into the sitting position.*

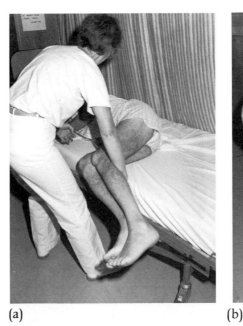
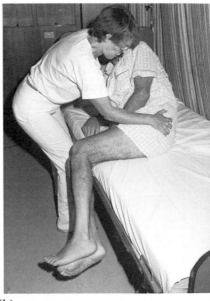

(a)                                        (b)

### To Assist Patient to Lie Down

*From the sitting position, patient shifts his weight down sideways on to his intact forearm. Therapist reminds him to move his head laterally in the opposite direction as she lifts his legs up on to the bed.*
*Patient lowers himself down on to his side.*

INSTRUCTIONS
'Lower yourself on to your arm.'
'Don't let your head flop down.'

CHECK
Do not pull on patient's arm.
Remind him to control his head position.
Do not let his weight go backwards.

### STEP 4   TRANSFERENCE OF TRAINING INTO DAILY LIFE

The patient should not spend any more time in bed than is necessary for medical reasons, nor should he spend any more time lying down than is necessary for sleeping or for the retraining of upper limb function in therapy sessions. The lying position reinforces drowsiness, confusion and feelings of helplessness, and provokes the symptoms of deprivation. Most patients early after stroke are helpless when in bed as their solitary attempts at movement are usually ineffectual. Early assumption of the erect position (i.e. sitting and standing) has a stimulating effect upon the central nervous system, counteracts depression, enables the patient to regain control over bladder function and oral function, gives relevant visual input and encourages communication. The person who appears virtually helpless in supine will usually be able to gain some control over the sitting position in one treatment session. It is therefore essential to assist him to sit up as soon as possible.

Should the patient need to remain in bed for medical reasons, he can be positioned as in Fig. 4.6. However, it is considered less effort for a patient to be assisted out of bed on to a commode than to use a bed pan. In addition, the sitting position appears to aid in emptying the bladder and bowel. If the patient *must* remain in bed, the task of getting on to a bedpan is made easier if the nurse flexes his affected hip and knee, holds his foot firmly on the bed and asks him to bend his intact hip and knee, push down through his heels and lift his buttocks (Fig. 4.7). This should not be attempted with more than one pillow under the head as a flexed position of head and trunk makes it difficult to extend the hips.

**Fig. 4.6 (a)** *The patient confined to bed is positioned on his side with a device for keeping bedclothes off his feet.* **(b)** *While sitting in bed his affected arm is supported on pillows.*

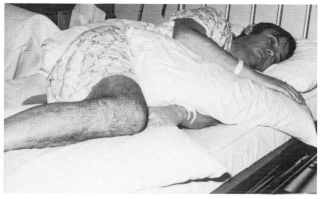

(a)

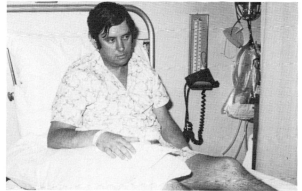

(b)

**Fig. 4.7** *If his affected leg is held steady at the knee and foot, this man can push down through his feet and lift his buttocks off the bed.*

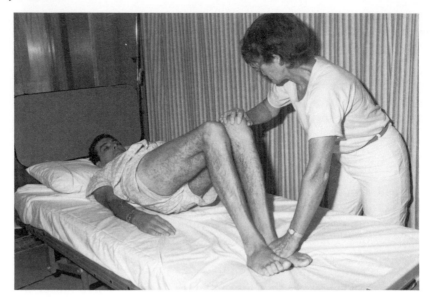

Nursing staff, therapists and relatives should follow the same procedure as given in this section when helping the patient out of bed in the morning and when helping him off the therapy bed, for as long as he needs assistance with this activity. The patient should not have a monkey ring suspended above his bed. Pulling down on a ring reinforces non-use of the affected side and emphasises overactivity of the intact upper limb.

## REFERENCES

1. Johnstone M. (1983). *Restoration of Motor Function in the Stroke Patient* 2nd edn. London: Churchill Livingstone.
2. Atkinson H. W. (1977). Principles of treatment (I & II). In *Neurology for Physiotherapists*, 2nd edn (Cash J., ed.) pp. 93–146 London: Faber & Faber.

# 5
# *Balanced sitting*

## DESCRIPTION OF NORMAL FUNCTION

The ability to be active in sitting requires that body alignment be appropriate to each task and that the correct preparatory and ongoing postural adjustments can be made as shifts in centre of gravity occur throughout performance of the task. At this point the reader should consult Appendix 5.

Balanced sitting is defined as the ability to sit without using undue muscle activity, to move about in sitting, to perform a wide variety of motor tasks (Fig. 5.1), and to move in and out of the sitting position. When one body segment moves, the position of the centre of gravity alters, and this requires movement of other segments in order to balance the body. Actual movements may or may not be easily observable, depending on the degree of displacement. However, even small shifts in centre of gravity (i.e. even slight movements of the head, trunk or limbs) involve some preparatory and ongoing muscle activity. Normally, weight is taken through the arms or hand for protective support only when the centre of gravity has moved so far that balance is lost.

## ESSENTIALS OF SITTING ALIGNMENT

Body alignment in sitting depends on a number of factors: (i) what one is sitting on; (ii) what one is doing; (iii) general body posture. If totally supported in an armchair, the body moulds itself to that chair and no postural adjustments are required unless one moves. In semi-supported situations we are rarely motionless, so alignment and the necessary postural adjustments are constantly changing. The following essentials of sitting alignment relate to sitting up straight.

- Feet and knees close together.
- Weight evenly distributed.
- Flexion of hips with extension of trunk (i.e. shoulders over hips).
- Head balanced on level shoulders.

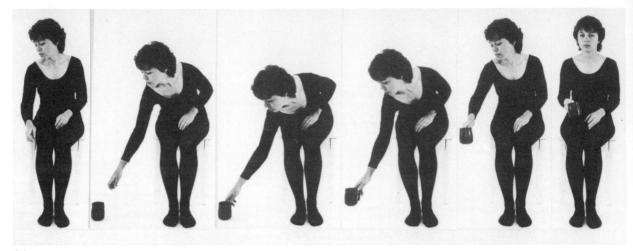

(a)

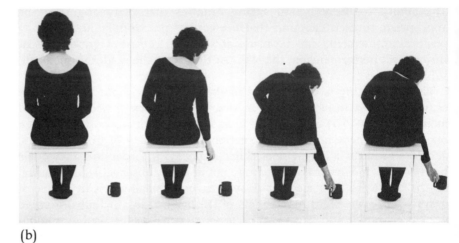

(b)

Fig. 5.1 (a) *and* (b) *Reaching to the floor for a cup. During these tasks, complex postural adjustments are made as part of the task.*

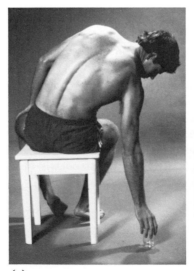

(a)

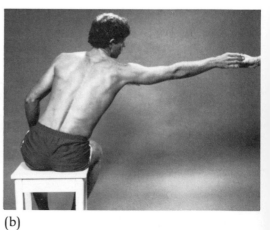

(b)

Fig. 5.2 (a) *and* (b) *Reaching sideways for a glass involves postural adjustments and limb movement which are specific to the task, in this case dependent on the position of the glass.*

## ESSENTIAL COMPONENTS OF BALANCED SITTING

The ability to make:

- preparatory postural adjustment, and
- ongoing postural adjustments which are specific to the movement or motor task being performed (Fig. 5.2).

### STEP 1    ANALYSIS OF BALANCED SITTING

Analysis of sitting consists of:

- observation of the patient's alignment in quiet sitting
- analysis of his ability to adjust to self-initiated movement of limbs, trunk and head as he performs a graded variety of motor tasks. Patient is asked, for example, to look at the ceiling, to turn and look behind him, to reach forward, sideways and backwards to touch or grasp an object, to lift his intact foot off the floor, to pick up an object from the floor.

The therapist notes his behaviour (Figs. 5.3 to 5.5), including extraneous movements and compensatory strategies, and analyses the reasons for any problems. Below is a list of some compensatory strategies which are commonly found in patients who are unbalanced in sitting.

- Wide base of support, i.e. feet and/or knees apart (Fig. 5.4).

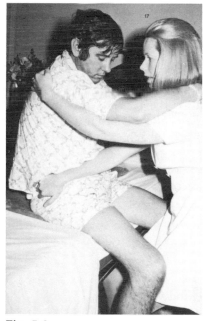

Fig. 5.3

Fig. 5.4

**Fig. 5.3** *This man has insufficient hip flexion. In compensation, his trunk and neck are flexed.*

**Fig. 5.4** *This man steadies himself by putting his legs apart and supporting himself on his hand.*

**Fig. 5.5** *This man leans forward as he reaches for the glass to compensate for his inability to move sideways. Note that even though he can achieve his goal, he would not be able to if the glass were placed further sideways or backwards.*

- Voluntary restriction of movement, i.e. patient holds himself stiffly and holds his breath.

- Patient shuffles feet instead of making adjustments with appropriate body segments.

- Protective support on hand or arm or grabbing for support with minimal movement. This patient may lose balance on any slight movement, even on taking a deep breath. He uses his hands to give himself a wider base and increase his stability (Fig. 5.4).

- Patient leans forwards or backwards when the task requires that body weight should be shifting sideways. This means lateral flexion of the trunk is poorly controlled (Fig. 5.5).

### STEPS 2 AND 3    PRACTICE OF BALANCED SITTING

During the first few sessions, if the patient's balance in sitting is poor, he should sit on a firm low bed (see Fig. 5.6) with his feet on the floor. As he progresses in his ability to move about, he should also practise various tasks while sitting on different types of seat. This training can be combined with training in standing up and sitting down.

As the patient practises moving about, the therapist ensures that he makes the necessary adjustments and does not shuffle his feet, widen his base or wriggle about. If the therapist holds him too much he will not *need* to adjust. She should avoid the use of phrases such as 'Don't let me push you', 'Resist me' and 'I'm going to threaten your balance', as these will encourage him to 'freeze', a response which very easily becomes habitual.

### To Train Postural Adjustments to Shifts in Centre of Gravity

NOTE
The first tasks are useful for the patient who, early after his stroke, is frightened of moving. They take his attention away from the need to balance by focusing his efforts on achieving a different goal.

*Sitting, hands in lap, patient turns head and trunk to look over his shoulder, returns to the mid position, repeats to the other side (Fig. 5.6).*

NOTE
This gives the opportunity to practise small adjustments. It shows the patient that he can move about independently, and enables him to regain a sense of balance.

INSTRUCTIONS
'Turn around and look behind you.'
'Turn your body as well as your head.'
'Don't lean back.'

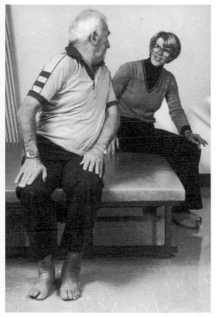
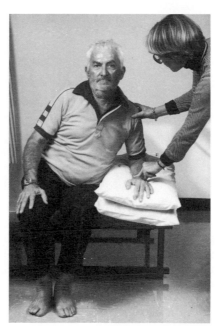

**Fig. 5.6** *Turning to look behind
requires a shift of centre of gravity
and gives the patient confidence in
his ability to move in a balanced
manner.*

**Fig. 5.7** *The patient practises
moving to the affected side and
sitting up again.*

Fig. 5.6                    Fig. 5.7

CHECK

Do not allow him to move his legs to one side unnecessarily. Make sure
he keeps his hands in his lap and his intact shoulder relaxed.

*In sitting, therapist assists patient sideways to support himself on the forearm
of his affected side on one or two pillows. Patient practises sitting up from
this position (Fig. 5.7).*

NOTE

This gives the patient the idea of how to control movement of trunk and
head in sitting and boosts his confidence in his ability to sit up.

INSTRUCTIONS

'Lower yourself on to the pillow.'
'Now, sit up.'

CHECK

Do not allow him to lean back.
Make sure his shoulder is over his elbow, and his head flexes laterally.

*Sitting, patient reaches forward to touch an object, downwards towards floor
and to both sides, each time returning to the upright position. Therapist supports the affected arm while necessary (Fig. 5.8).*

INSTRUCTIONS

'Reach out and touch . . .'
'Look at the object.'
'Now, sit up again.'
'Let's do it again—come on—see if you can reach a little further.'
'Stay there a little longer—now, go back slowly.'

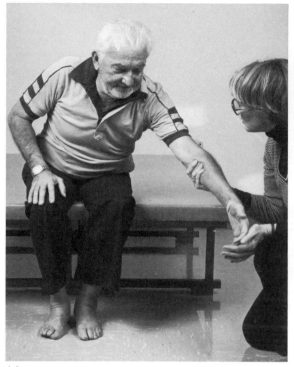

(a)

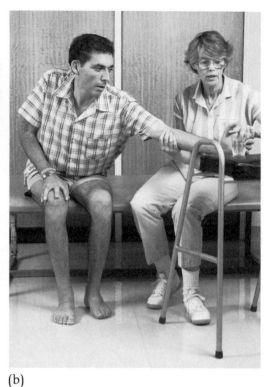

(b)

**Fig. 5.8a** *Therapist supports this man's affected arm while he reaches to touch her hand.*

**Fig. 5.8b** *This man reaches out to the glass. Therapist supports his flaccid arm so that he can concentrate on moving his body sideways and forwards.*

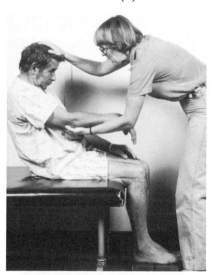

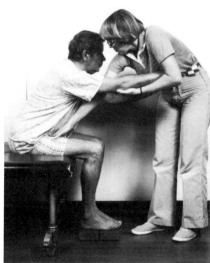

**Fig. 5.8c** *The therapist has instructed this man to flex his spine and head, thus controlling his movement backwards.*

**Fig. 5.8d** *The therapist indicates to him that he must flex at his hips and not at his spine in order to move forward.*

CHECK
Point out necessary adjustments to be made.
Make sure to correct head and trunk movement.
Direct patient's eyes towards a target.
Keep drawing patient's attention towards his affected side, making sure he has his weight on this side when appropriate.
Make sure he does not rush the difficult part of the activity.

NOTE
If the patient falls persistently towards the affected side, the therapist will often tend to concentrate on having him move towards the intact side in the hope that this will enable him to balance himself. However, it is usually more effective to encourage him to reach out moving towards his *affected* side (Fig. 5.8a and b). The effectiveness of this solution may result from him being given a strategy for **controlling** movement to the affected side, rather than a strategy for **compensating** for his tendency to fall to that side. Similarly, if a patient has a tendency to fall backwards, he can be encouraged to control movement in this direction and given practice in moving both backwards and forwards (Fig. 5.8c and d).

## To Increase Complexity

The patient's ability to balance must be continually expanded by the addition to his programme of more complex activities, such as:

*Sitting, reaching sideways and downwards to pick up an object from the floor (Fig. 5.9).*

NOTE
This can be made easier by putting the object on a book, for example, and harder by putting the object further away in a sideways or backwards direction.

CHECK
Patient must go sideways and not forward.

*Sitting, picking up a light box from the floor with both hands. Sitting, reaching forward to pick up an object from a table with both hands.*

*Sitting, reaching backwards to pick up an object (Fig. 5.10).*

NOTE
If the patient lacks sufficient hand control, he should try to touch the object.

STEP 4    TRANSFERENCE OF TRAINING INTO DAILY LIFE

It is the authors' experience that the majority of people trained in the manner proposed in this section become balanced in sitting within a very

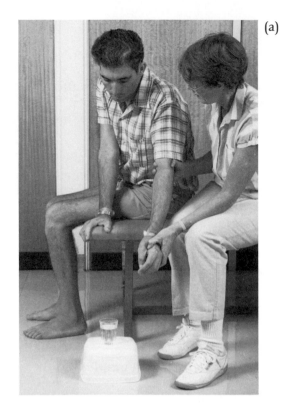

(a)

**Fig. 5.9 (a)** *Note this man's compensatory strategies as he reaches towards the glass.* **(b)** *The therapist encourages him to reach sideways and touch the glass, supporting his affected arm. Note that he moves forward to compensate for difficulty moving sideways.* **(c)** *Now he does better and is gaining some control over the sideways movement required by the task. He needs to be reminded not to hold on to his R. knee.*

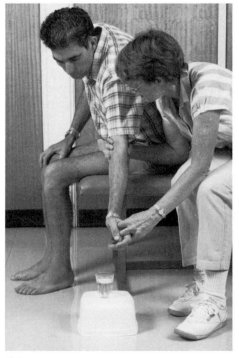

(b)

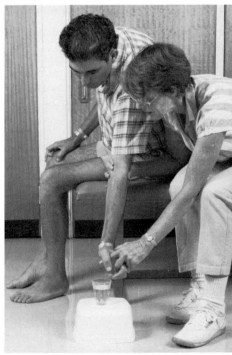

(c)

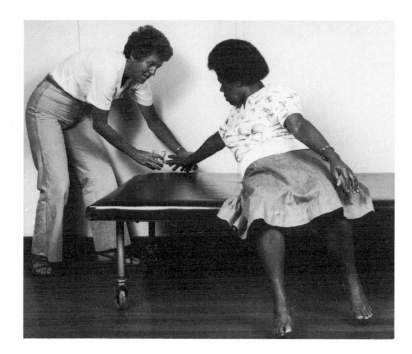

**Fig. 5.10** *Therapist moves glass to the outer limits of this R. hemiplegic person's range. She does not move it so far that the woman loses control and overbalances.*

short period (usually a few days). Emphasis in Step 4 is therefore on organising for the resting posture of the flaccid arm to be varied throughout the day and for the patient to have the opportunity to practise standing up.

Throughout the day, whenever the patient is sitting, he should sit on a chair from which it is possible for him to stand up (with assistance if necessary). Chairs provided for stroke patients frequently enforce passivity. A compromise should be achieved between comfort and ease of standing up (see p. 109). The patient should remember to shift his weight from one buttock to the other from time to time. If his arm is flaccid, it should be supported on a table. In this position, he will be able to read and do other activities. The patient can be given his own check list with some major points for practice throughout the day, for example turning his body to look around him.

## FURTHER READING

See references in Appendix 5.

# 6

# *Standing up and sitting down*

## DESCRIPTION OF NORMAL FUNCTION

The movement organisation of standing up varies according to the goal, which may not be merely to stand up but rather to walk out of the room or shake hands with a friend. Both standing up and sitting down involve shifting the body mass from one base of support to another with minimal expenditure of energy.

In **standing up**, one or both feet are moved backwards. This gives a base under the centre of gravity as it is moved forward. Inclination of the extended trunk forward at the hips with forward movement of the knees brings the centre of gravity over the feet and enables the weight of the body to be shifted forward and upwards (Fig. 6.1). If the chair prevents the feet from moving far enough backwards, the trunk has to incline further forward or one has to move nearer the edge of the chair.

It is important to consider the trajectories of knees and shoulders (that is, the paths through which they move) since observation of these is helpful for the therapist both in analysis of dysfunction and in training control over the task. Figure 6.2, taken from a kinematic analysis of standing up,[1] illustrates these as well as the angular displacement of hips, knees and ankles.

**Fig. 6.1 (a)** *and* **(b)** *Standing up. Note the components and the sequence in which they occur.*

(a)

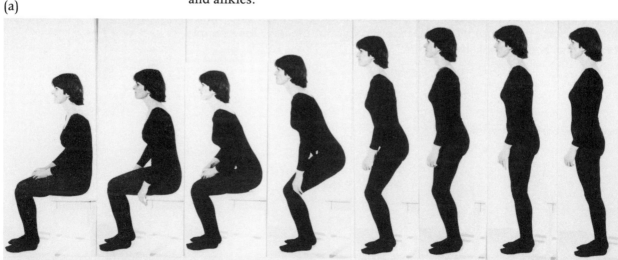

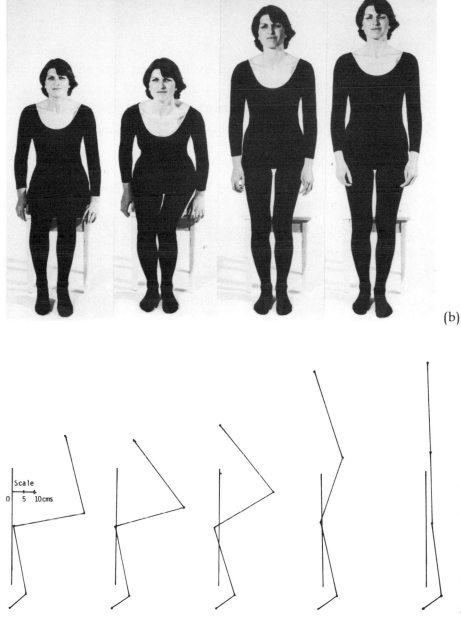

(b)

**Fig. 6.2** *Stick figures (made from XY co-ordinates taken from high-speed film) show the trajectories of knee and the angular displacement of ankle, hip and knee at certain points in the sequence of standing up. (Note that the ankle marker is actually over the lateral malleolus and the foot is flat on the floor.)*

In **sitting down**, one normally checks the whereabouts of the chair by turning to look, feeling for the chair with the hand or feeling it against the back of the leg. The hips and knees flex, the trunk is inclined forward so that the centre of gravity can be shifted backwards. The body weight is lowered to the chair by a lengthening or eccentric contraction of the extensor muscles. It is the forward inclination of the trunk caused by flexion of the hips and the forward movement of the knees which enable the pelvis to move backwards and downwards towards the chair.

ESSENTIAL COMPONENTS

1. **Standing up.**

    - Foot placement.

    - Inclination of trunk forward by flexion at hips with extended neck and spine.

    - Movement of the knees forward.

    - Extension of hips and knees for final standing alignment.

2. **Sitting down.**

    - Inclination of trunk forward by flexion at hips with extended neck and spine.

    - Movement of the knees forward.

    - Knee flexion.

STEP 1   ANALYSIS OF STANDING UP AND SITTING DOWN

The therapist observes the patient's body alignment throughout the task, or his attempts at the task. Note that symmetrical weight distribution and a narrow base of support are not considered to be essential components of standing up and sitting down as there are many environmental and motivational factors which will influence these. However, the stroke patient, because of his lack of force-generating capacity in his affected leg, is compelled to shift his weight on to his intact leg when he attempts to stand up and sit down and this will soon become a learned compensatory strategy.

The common problems are as follows.

- Weight is borne principally through the intact side (Fig. 6.3).

- Inability to shift centre of gravity sufficiently forward (Fig. 6.4 and 6.5a), i.e. failure to move shoulders forward over feet and move knees forward.

- Patient tries to shift weight forward by flexing trunk and head instead of hips (Fig. 6.5b) or by wriggling forward to the edge of the chair.

- Failure to place the affected foot ensures that the patient, who already has this tendency, will stand up and sit down with all weight taken through the intact foot (Fig. 6.3).

Fig. 6.3

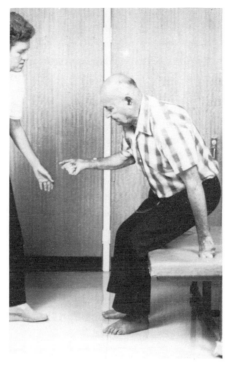

Fig. 6.4

**Fig. 6.3** *This man's weight is principally on his intact R. side. His base of support is wide for the task. His L. foot has not been placed back.*

**Fig. 6.4** *This man cannot stand up unaided as he cannot shift his body weight forward. Note his knees and shoulders have not moved far enough forward and he is attempting to straighten his hips and knees too soon.*

**Fig. 6.5a** *In sitting down, this woman is attempting to flex her hips and knees with her body weight too far behind her base of support. Note her knees and shoulders are not far enough forward. Foot position suggests that she has more weight on her R. leg than her L.*

**Fig. 6.5b** *This woman is sitting down. She is unable to incline her trunk sufficiently forward at her hips and move her knees forward. She flexes her head and upper trunk in compensation and uses her arms to counterbalance her tendency to fall backward.*

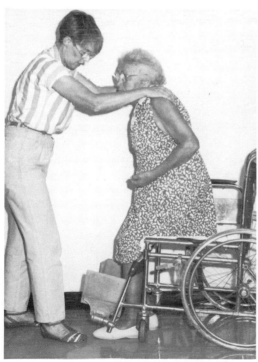

Fig. 6.5a

Fig. 6.5b

STEP 2    PRACTICE OF MISSING COMPONENTS

### To Train Trunk Inclination Forward at Hips (with Knee Movement Forward)

*In sitting, feet flat on floor, patient practises inclining his trunk forward by flexing at the hips with the neck and trunk extended (Fig. 6.6), with enough momentum to move the knees forward. He should aim to push down and back through his feet.*

NOTE
The patient may rest his arms on the therapist's waist if necessary. The therapist elevates affected shoulder to preserve body alignment (i.e. keep shoulders level). She may need to place the patient's affected foot under the stool if he cannot do it himself.

INSTRUCTIONS
'Move your shoulders in front of your feet and push down and back through your feet.'
'Push down more through this (affected) foot.'
'Look straight ahead.'

CHECK
Avoid phrases such as 'Lean forward', 'Take your head to your toes', as these will encourage the patient to move incorrectly.

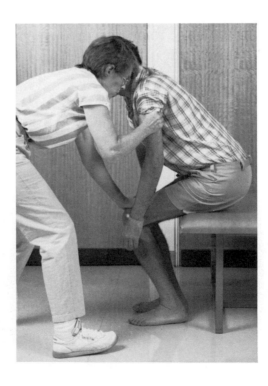

**Fig. 6.6** *A few days after his stroke, this man has the idea of what he must do to stand up (i.e. the knee and shoulder trajectories). He is practising to the point of thighs-off. The therapist is assisting him to do the first part of the movement by keeping his L. knee forward and pushing down through his knee. This anchors his foot to the floor and gives him the idea of movement.*

Do not stand too close to the patient as this will interfere with the shoulder and knee trajectories and the shift of the centre of gravity forward.

Do not stand in a position which prevents the patient bearing weight through the affected side.

## STEP 3    PRACTICE OF STANDING UP AND SITTING DOWN

### Standing Up

If the patient is very weak, overweight, or unable to generate sufficient force to stand up, he may need two people to assist him to stand up (Fig. 6.7a).

Practice of standing up may be facilitated by the use of a higher chair (Fig. 6.7b) which eliminates some of the difficulty involved in generating force. Patients who have difficulty standing up may find it easier to gain some muscle control as they sit down, and practice of sitting down (an eccentric contraction of the extensors) will enable them to improve control over the more difficult action of standing up.

**Fig. 6.7a** *This photograph illustrates how two people can assist a patient to stand ensuring the appropriate angular displacements.* **Note**: *the patient is not lifted into standing.*

**Fig. 6.7b** *A higher than normal chair enables this man to stand with minimum assistance from the therapist.*

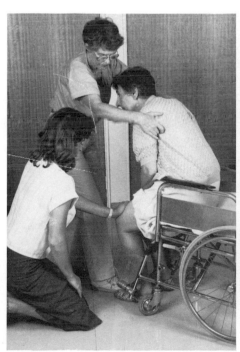

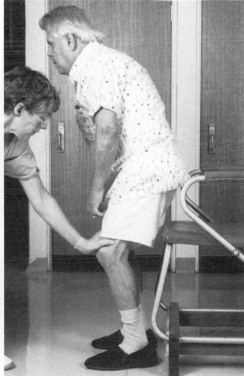

(a)                              (b)

*With his shoulders and knees forward, the patient practises standing up. The therapist can give him the idea of pushing down through his affected foot by pushing down through his knee along the line of the shank while moving it forward (Fig. 6.8a and b).*

NOTE

The therapist can also assist the patient by giving some manual guidance at the shoulder (see Fig. 6.10). Initially, it may be helpful for the patient to rest his arms at the therapist's waist. This is to enable the therapist to give him a little support. However, he must use his legs to stand up and not pull around the therapist's waist. In standing up, at the point where weight is being shifted on to the foot, the quadriceps contracts to move the thigh on the shank and the dorsiflexor muscles contract to move the shank on the foot. These two muscle groups are probably that part of the synergy which ensures that force is generated downwards and backwards. The therapist brings the knee forward in order that the angular alignment is appropriate and pushes down through the knee in order to assist the patient to keep his foot in contact with the floor. If this latter does not occur, contraction of the quadriceps will cause the shank to move on the thigh and the foot to slide forward and lift from the floor.

**Fig. 6.8 (a)** *This patient is standing up with assistance but his body weight is too far behind his base of support (note his extended toes).* **(b)** *The therapist guides his L. knee forward more than in* **(a)** *and allows his shoulders also to move forward. His body alignment is now appropriate for the task. Note the excessively elevated shoulder in* **(a)**, *demonstrating a major problem inherent in the placing of the patient's affected arm on the therapist's shoulder.*

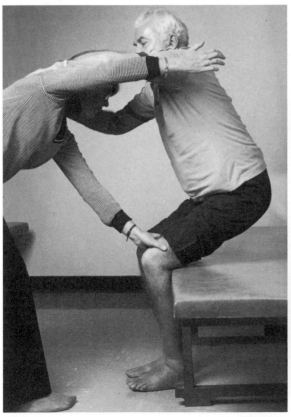

(a)

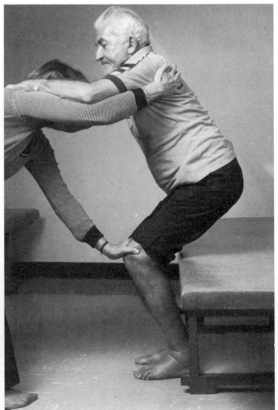

(b)

INSTRUCTIONS
'Press down through your (affected) foot and stand up.'
When he is standing : 'Bring your hips forward/towards me.'

CHECK
Make sure some weight is taken through the affected foot.
Do not wedge your knee against the patient's knee while he is standing up as this interferes with the forward movement of the knee.
Do not let the patient move to the edge of the chair to compensate for lack of forward inclination of the trunk when the chair is of the correct height and there is room for the feet to move back.
Do not extend the knee passively backwards when it should be shifting forward (Fig. 6.9).
Make sure the patient does as much of the task as he can.
Make sure the shoulders move far enough forward.

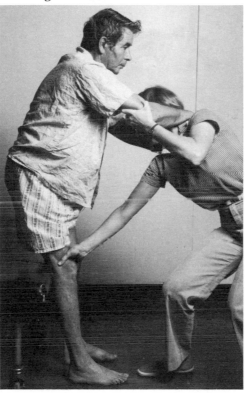

**Fig. 6.9** *The therapist demonstrates how, in straightening the patient's knee passively and too soon, she puts him off balance backwards and* **prevents** *him from extending his hips and bringing his centre of gravity forward.*

**Sitting Down**

*The reverse of standing up (Fig. 6.10). The therapist may need to help the patient with the forward movement of the shoulders and knees at the beginning of the movement. The therapist keeps the weight on the affected leg as the patient sits down by pushing down through his knee.*

INSTRUCTIONS
'Move your bottom down and back and sit down.'
'Move your knees forward.'

**Fig. 6.10** *Practice of sitting down. The therapist guides the movement to ensure the shoulders move forward.* **(a)** *Patient rests arms on the therapist's waist.* **(b)** *Therapist guides at the shoulders.*

(a)

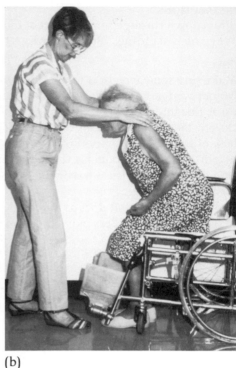

(b)

CHECK

Do not stand too close to the patient or hold his arms in such a way as to interfere with the forward movement of shoulders and knees.
Make sure some weight is borne through the affected foot.

## To Increase Complexity

*Patient practises standing up and sitting down, stopping in different parts of the range, changing direction and altering speed. The therapist directs these spatial and temporal variations (Fig. 6.11).*

Standing up and sitting down is normally performed in everyday life under variable environmental conditions. To train the patient to be flexible and adaptable, a variety of conditions should be introduced: for example, standing up from different surfaces, walking off to one side, holding an object, talking. If he understands the strategies for getting his centre of gravity over his changing base of support and he has the chance to practise, he will soon learn to adapt to changing task and environmental demands.

**STEP 4** TRANSFERENCE OF TRAINING INTO DAILY LIFE

There is a great improvement both in morale and lifestyle when a person can stand up from a chair unaided by another. The patient has to be

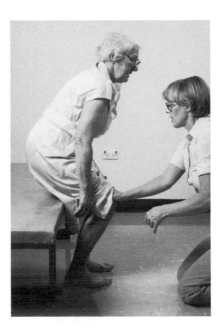

**Fig. 6.11** *The therapist helps this woman to shift her knee forward and take weight through her affected leg while standing up and sitting down.*

able to stand up and sit down by himself in order to change from one chair to another, to go to the toilet and to practise walking. To become efficient in this task he needs the opportunity to practise on his own. This will require that the therapist organises a written checklist of what he is to practise and what specific goals he is to achieve. These could include, for example, the number of repetitions to be completed a certain number of times each day, or a particular component on which to concentrate. The patient can practise at a table (Fig. 6.12), inclining the trunk forward and pushing down through his heels to get the idea of lifting his thighs off the chair.

One way of making this task of standing up easier is to provide a higher chair (see Fig. 6.7b). Naumann and colleagues[2] found that increasing the seat height to 150% of calcaneo-tibial length decreased knee shear force by 60%. Burdett and colleagues[3] compared the joint moments and range of motion of 10 healthy male subjects and 4 male subjects with lower extremity musculoskeletal disability rising from a standard chair, with a seat height of 43 cm, and from a specially designed chair (E-Z Up Artherapedic Chair*), with a seat height of 64 cm, with and without the use of arms to assist standing up. Results of this study demonstrate that standing up from a higher chair reduces the stress on hip and knee. The joint moments needed were significantly decreased, indicating that less muscle activity is needed. The range of motion was also significantly reduced. Some patients will not be able to stand up unaided without the provision of such a chair.

Standing up from a chair specially designed to be comfortable for the elderly was shown, in a study by Wheeler and colleagues,[4] to be more

* Alda Industries Inc., 214 Harvard Ave., Allston, MA 02134, USA.

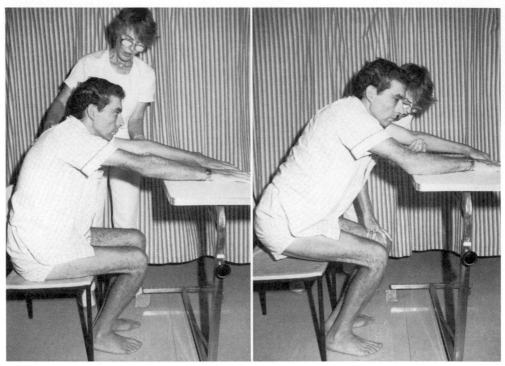

**Fig. 6.12** *This man is being taught how he can practise the first part of standing up (to thighs-off) using a table to indicate how far his shoulders should move forward.*

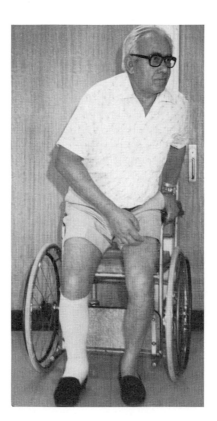

**Fig. 6.13** *Note how this man's weight and attention are directed towards his intact side when he uses his intact arm to push himself up into standing.*

difficult than standing up from a standard armchair, indicating that although a chair may be designed for comfort in sitting, it may in fact make standing up unaided more difficult, or impossible.

Members of staff and the patient's relatives need to understand the basic biomechanical principles involved, how to assist the patient and how to reinforce and monitor his performance. Particularly in this task, there is a tendency for the patient to practise standing up one way while with the therapist in the physiotherapy area and for him to stand up another way in other environments or on his own (Fig. 6.13). Some training sessions with the therapist in these other environments may help overcome this problem.

A major point in motor training is consistency of practice. There is no consistency if the patient practises one way in therapy and another way throughout the day. The therapist should know that what he practises is what he will learn.

## REFERENCES

1. Canning C., Carr J. H. and Shepherd R. B. (1985). *A Kinematic Analysis of Standing Up*. Proceedings of Australian Physiotherapy Association Conference, Brisbane.
2. Naumann S., Ziv I. and Rang M. C. (1982). Biomechanics of standing up from a chair. In *Human Locomotion II: Proceedings of the Second Biannual Conference of the Canadian Society for Biomechanics*, pp. 78–79. University of Ottowa, Canada.
3. Burdett R. G., Habasevich R., Pisciotta J. and Simon S. R. (1985). Biomechanical comparison of rising from two types of chairs *Phys. Ther*; **65**: 1177–83.
4. Wheeler J., Woodward D., Usovich R. L., Perry J. and Walker J. M. (1985). Rising from a chair. Influence of age and chair design. *Phys. Ther*; **65**: 22–6.

# 7

# *Balanced standing*

## DESCRIPTION OF NORMAL FUNCTION

The ability to be active in standing requires that body alignment be appropriate throughout quiet standing and for each task being performed in this position, and that the correct preparatory and ongoing adjustments can be made as shifts in centre of gravity occur.

Balanced standing involves the ability to stand relatively still without using undue muscular activity, to move about in standing to perform a wide variety of tasks (Fig. 7.1), to move in and out of the standing position, and to take steps. Standing is not a static posture but involves constant slight movements, called 'postural sway'. Even small shifts of centre of gravity (i.e. even slight movements of the head, thorax or limbs) involve some preparatory and ongoing muscle activity.

Body alignment is more critical in standing than in sitting since the base of support is so small. A well-aligned position requires less energy

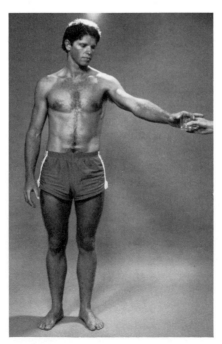

**Fig. 7.1** *Reaching to take a glass involves preparatory and ongoing postural adjustments which are specific to the task.*

than a poorly aligned position. The most balanced position for standing is with the feet a few inches apart so that the legs are vertical. This gives the best base of support, not so large or so small that it introduces a diagonal force against the ground. In the sagittal plane, the shoulders should be directly above the hips and the hips just in front of the ankles. This initial alignment of body segments allows the person to move about and function effectively because he is well enough balanced to do so. Of course, as in sitting, body alignment in standing depends on a number of factors, including: (i) what one is standing on (for example floor, ramp, deck of a moving boat); (ii) what one is doing (for example leaning on a table, standing in line, waiting for a serve in tennis); (iii) one's general body posture, and other factors such as age and sex. The reader should refer to Appendix 5 for more information on adjustments to gravity.

### ESSENTIALS OF STANDING ALIGNMENT

- Feet a few inches apart.
- Hips in front of ankles.
- Shoulders over hips.
- Head balanced on level shoulders.
- Erect trunk.

### ESSENTIAL COMPONENTS OF BALANCED STANDING

The ability to make

- preparatory postural adjustments, and
- ongoing postural adjustments

which are specific to the goal of either standing still or performing particular motor tasks.

### STEP 1    ANALYSIS OF BALANCED STANDING

Analysis of standing consists of the following.

- Observation of the patient's alignment in quiet standing (Fig. 7.2).
- Analysis of his ability to adjust to self-initiated movements of limbs, trunk and head as he performs a graded variety of motor tasks. The patient is asked, for example, to look up at the ceiling, to look behind him, to reach forward, sideways and backwards to touch or grasp an object, to stand on one leg, to pick up an object from the floor.

**Fig. 7.2** *This woman lacks hip and knee extension, i.e. her segmental alignment is abnormal.*

**Fig. 7.3** *Note how stiffly this woman holds herself, with her weight more on the R. side than the L., on one of her first attempts to stand alone.*

**Fig. 7.4 (a)** *and* **(b)** *These men both demonstrate a wide base of support. The man in* **(b)** *has given himself a wider base by externally rotating his L. leg.*

Fig. 7.3                    Fig. 7.4a                    Fig. 7.4b

The therapist notes his behaviour (Figs. 7.3 and 7.4), including compensatory strategies, and analyses the reason for any problems. Below is a list of some compensatory strategies which are commonly found in patients with poor balance.

- Wide base of support, i.e. feet too far apart or one or both hips externally rotated (Fig. 7.4).

- Voluntary restriction of movement, i.e. patient holds himself stiffly and holds his breath (Fig. 7.3).

- Patient shuffles feet instead of making adjustments with the appropriate body segments.

- Patient takes a step prematurely, i.e. as soon as centre of gravity moves. This means that balance is lost too soon on only slight movement.

- Patient flexes at hips instead of dorsiflexing at ankles in reaching forward (see Fig. 7.14), and moves at trunk instead of hips and feet in reaching sideways (Fig. 7.5).

- Use of arms, i.e. grabbing for support, holding arms out sideways or forward, on minimal shift of centre of gravity.

### STEPS 2 AND 3    PRACTICE OF BALANCED STANDING

All stroke patients when they first attempt to stand are off balance. Many

**Fig. 7.5** *When this man reaches sideways he does not shift his weight sufficiently over the R. leg and so must bend at the waist in order to achieve his goal.*

of them tend to drift to one side or fall backwards. Many patients react by shifting most of their weight on to the intact side. From the start, the patient must understand what is going wrong and how to correct it. He must know that the solution does not lie in holding on with his hands but in gaining control over his pelvis, legs and trunk. Similarly, the therapist must not panic and react by holding him up. If she resists this impulse and gives him a strategy for overcoming the problem, for example 'Bring your hips in front of your ankles' (with verbal feedback and manual guidance), he will quickly learn to make an effective adjustment himself.

It is important that the patient stands within the first few days and with weight through both legs. This enables him to commence training in balancing and walking skills. A rapid regaining of balance in standing increases awareness of bilaterality, and position in space and of body parts, which is particularly important for people with unilateral spatial neglect or diminished kinaesthetic sensation. Standing prevents contracture, particularly of the calf muscles and hip flexor muscles, provides motivation and encouragement, and, as balance improves, self-confidence; in the early stages it increases the level of alertness and probably influences bladder control. Standing with weight through the affected leg in correct alignment may be one of the factors in minimising the development of spasticity in the leg.

Some patients, due to unilateral spatial neglect or inability to contract their leg muscles, will find it easier to stand if the knee is controlled in a **calico splint** (see p. 117). The **limb load monitor**\* may enable the

\* Krusen Research Center, Philadelphia, Pennsylvania, USA.

patient to get the 'idea' of taking weight through his affected foot.

The relative importance of balance in different positions is often misunderstood in rehabilitation. There is no evidence of a 'sequence' of balance activity in adults in the sense sometimes espoused in neurodevelopmental theory. Recent research has demonstrated that postural adjustments (and therefore muscle activity) are probably task specific (and posture specific). Hence, practice of balanced sitting should not be expected to transfer into balanced standing. It is also probable that, following a stroke, a person will not automatically regain the ability to move about in standing with the necessary postural adjustments without specific training in standing. Hence, to postpone standing because a person 'has no balance' makes little sense.

### To Train Hip Alignment

*Supine, leg over side of the bed, patient practises small-range hip extension* (Fig. 7.6).

INSTRUCTIONS
'Push your heel gently down to the floor and lift your hip up a little.'
'Don't lift your hip too high.'

CHECK
Make sure the thigh is aligned correctly, i.e. that the hip is not too abducted or internally rotated. Knee should be at a right-angle or less.
Discourage him from plantarflexing his foot.
Make sure he does not move or tense up his intact side.
Push down through his knee to give him the idea of the movement.

Fig. 7.6 (a) *This man is unable to extend his hip and knee and therefore cannot take weight through his leg.* (b) *The therapist, having decided that hip extension is the major missing component, trains the patient to contract his hip extensors.*

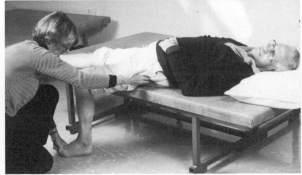

(a)                              (b)

Followed by:

*Patient stands with weight on both feet and hips extended (Fig. 7.7).*

NOTE

He is assisted to stand up with weight on both feet, as on p. 106. The improved alignment of the pelvis on the leg which results from the above technique usually enables the patient to develop some knee control. If the tendency for the knee to flex remains a problem, he should wear a calico splint (see below).

INSTRUCTIONS

'Push down through your feet and stand up.'
'Bring your hips towards me/forward over your feet.'
'Keep your weight over on this (affected) foot'.

## To Prevent The Knee From Flexing

NOTE

Difficulty controlling the knee in the first few days is often a major factor in delaying standing activities. A calico splint (Fig. 7.8), put on in standing, enables the patient to bear weight through the affected leg without having to worry about his knee collapsing and allows him to stand and learn to make the necessary postural adjustments as he performs simple tasks (Fig. 7.9). He will be able to practise stepping forward with the intact leg, walking sideways, and many of the motor tasks described below. Standing in the calico splint enables the patient to gain some muscular control of the extended knee, and the splint may only have to be worn for one or two sessions. An added advantage of the splint is to enable the therapist to commence training a patient who would otherwise find the task of standing very difficult. The person with unilateral spatial neglect, whose subjective midpoint has shifted towards the intact

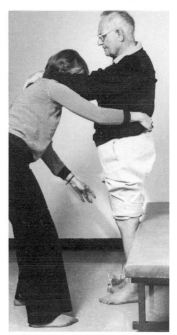

Fig. 7.7 *After a few minutes practice of activating his hip extensors, he is able to stand with weight through the L. leg with the leg in normal alignment.*

Fig. 7.8 (a) *Calico splint made from a double layer of 80% duck, with two aluminium struts and Velcro straps.* (b) *Pattern for calico splint.*

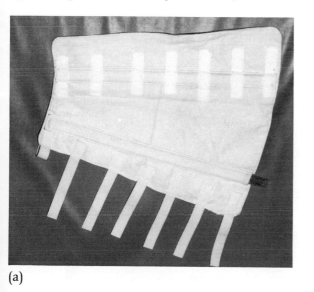

(a)

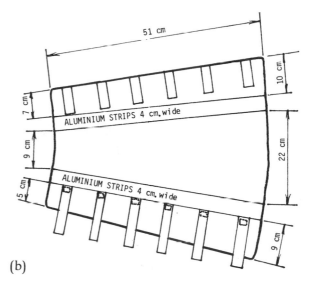

(b)

**Fig. 7.9** *This woman is practising standing with her weight on the affected foot while controlling hip position. The splint allows both her and the therapist to concentrate on the task.*

side, may find it impossible to bear weight through the affected leg without a calico splint.

### To Elicit Quadriceps Contraction

If the patient cannot activate his quadriceps, he needs to practise this specifically.

*Sitting with his knee supported in extension, he should practise 'moving his knee cap' and sustaining a quadriceps contraction for as long as he can (Fig. 7.10); sitting with his knee held in extension by the therapist, he should try to prevent the foot from falling to the ground, and/or let his foot down slowly when the therapist 'lets go' of his leg; EMG biofeedback with a visual or auditory display will provide motivation and more explicit feedback.*

Specific control over knee musculature is also trained in the manner described on p. 136.

### To Train Postural Adjustments to Shifts in Centre of Gravity

NOTE

The therapist should avoid the use of such phrases as 'Don't let me push you', 'Resist me', or 'I'm going to threaten your balance', as these will encourage the patient to 'freeze', a response which very quickly becomes habitual. She must be careful not to hold the patient so much that no motor activity is necessary. However, she should not allow him to over-balance. He should practise the tasks listed below just within the limits of his ability, trying always to extend these limits. This means that the therapist constantly monitors his body alignment to ensure that it is appropriate to the task being attempted. He is actively discouraged from holding on or reaching out for support. He is told to use his legs to balance,

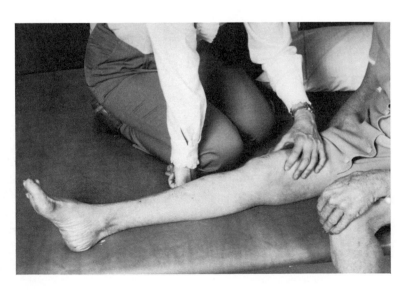

**Fig. 7.10** *This woman practises contracting her quadriceps in their shortened position and sustaining the contraction to counting.*

not his hands or arms. If the patient tends to 'freeze' or stiffen, as he may do if he feels his balance is at risk, the therapist can use the first few tasks described below to improve his confidence. These tasks demonstrate to him that he can move in a balanced manner with only a little assistance or guidance.

*Standing with feet a few inches apart, the patient looks up at the ceiling (Fig. 7.11).*

INSTRUCTIONS

'Look up at the ceiling—don't just move your eyes. You won't fall over.'
'Bring your hips forward.'
'Move forward at your ankles as you look up.'

CHECK

Correct his tendency to fall backwards by reminding him to move his hips.
Discourage him from grabbing hold of you.
Discourage him from moving his feet.

*Standing with feet a few inches apart, the patient turns his head and trunk to look behind him, returns to the mid position, and repeats to the other side (Fig. 7.12a). He should progress to doing this with one foot in front (Fig. 7.12b).*

INSTRUCTIONS

'Turn around and look behind you—turn your body as well as your head.'
'Don't move your feet.'

**Fig. 7.11** *The same woman as in Fig. 7.3 as she successfully looks up at the ceiling without falling backwards.*

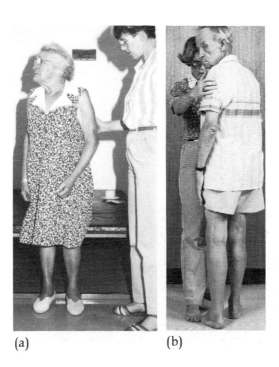

(a)  (b)

**Fig. 7.12a** *Now she turns to look behind her. The therapist's hand is ready to assist if she falls backwards instead of making the necessary preparatory and ongoing postural adjustments.*

**Fig. 7.12b** *With one foot in front, the patient turns to look behind. Therapist steadies him with her hands.*

CHECK
Make sure standing alignment is preserved.
Do not allow patient to shift his feet. If necessary, place your foot next to his.

*Standing, reaching forward, sideways and backward to take an object from a table, and a variety of reaching and pointing tasks offering a degree of challenge (Figs. 7.13 to 7.15).*

NOTE
Reaching tasks are practised with feet a few inches apart at first and then one foot in front.

INSTRUCTIONS
'See if you can touch this. Come on, just a little further.'
'Don't shift your feet.'
'Push down through your L. foot as you reach over to the R.'

CHECK
Make sure he is not expected to reach a distance at which it would be normal to take a step.
Encourage him to 'loosen up' and not hold himself stiffly.
Make sure he moves his body on his feet where this is required for the task.

*Patient takes a step forward with the intact leg, then backwards.*

INSTRUCTIONS
'Keep your weight on this (affected) foot.'
'Take a step forward with your other foot.'
'Your hip should move in front of your foot.'
'Now, step backwards.'

**Fig. 7.13a** *Compare this with Fig. 7.3 and note how she is now able to reach out for a glass with some confidence.*

Fig. 7.13b

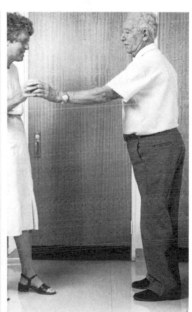

Fig. 7.14

**Fig. 7.13b Left.** *This man is reluctant to shift to the L. too far so he compensates by turning his body and bending forward at the hips.*
**Centre.** *Therapist gives him the idea of shifting more weight to the L. leg.*
**Right.** *Now he can practise.*

**Fig. 7.14 Left.** *He does not shift at his ankles in reaching forward, and compensates by flexing at his hips and increasing the amount of shoulder girdle protraction and trunk rotation. This man had a tendency to fall backwards whenever he moved in standing and was very unsteady on his feet.*
**Centre.** *Therapist shows him how to move his body forward so his hips are in front of his ankles.* **Right.** *Now he has the idea and can practise.*

**Fig. 7.15** *Reaching backwards to pick up a glass.*

CHECK

Do not allow hip on affected side to flex. It must extend as he steps forward with the intact leg.

Do not allow patient to shift pelvis too far laterally.

When patient steps forward, make sure he does not step too far to the side.

NOTE

If necessary, patient can rest his arms on the therapist's shoulders or waist. This gives him a little support. Therapist should encourage him to keep shoulders level.

A particular problem with many patients is an inability to control a weight shift backwards by dorsi flexing the ankles. This is usually compensated for by excessive leaning forward at the hips. There may be several reasons for the problem, including tight calf muscles or inability to bring the hips forward over the feet, and intervention will need to address these specific causes. However, if lack of active dorsiflexion is a cause, the following training method may help the patient to get the idea of the movement.

*Patient stands with back against a wall, feet a few inches away from it. He holds his arms out in front with hands together. Therapist holds his hands. The patient moves his hips away from the wall and the therapist gives either slight resistance or assistance to guide the movement and ensure that his weight remains backwards. During the backwards and forward movement, the therapist looks for the point at which dorsiflexor activity is elicited and then confines the patient's active movements around this point (Fig. 7.16).*

INSTRUCTIONS

'Bring your bottom away from the wall.'

'There, see how you are lifting your toes up a little. Try to lift them up a little more.'

CHECK

Do not allow patient to pull with his arms. He should move away from the wall with extended elbows, using his legs.

Make sure his weight is on both feet.

Ensure that his knees do not flex.

Hips should stay behind ankles throughout.

### To Increase Complexity

The patient's ability to function in standing must be continually expanded by the addition to the Programme of more complex activities. These may vary from talking to the therapist while standing with a narrow base to bimanual activities in standing. Below are some examples.

*Catching a ball thrown in such a way as to require him to reach sideways, forward and downwards, and to step out to catch it.*

(a)

(b)

(c)

**Fig. 7.16 (a)** *When he leans back against the wall, this man does not dorsiflex his L. foot.* **(b)** *and* **(c)** *The therapist is making him move back and forth concentrating on using his ankle dorsiflexors.*

*Picking up from the floor different sized objects with one hand and/or bimanually (Fig. 7.17).*

*Practice of walking improves balance, and variety and complexity can be added by having the patient stop when asked, change direction, step over objects.*

**Fig. 7.17** *Picking up a glass from the floor. He should now go on to practise picking up a box from the floor with two hands.*

### STEP 4    TRANSFERENCE OF TRAINING INTO DAILY LIFE

The patient should be helped to stand up and should begin training in standing from his first therapy session if his medical condition is satisfactory. He should also have the opportunity to practise during the day. He should know to stand with his body segments aligned correctly and with weight borne through the affected leg. He should be given written instructions of the major points so that he can monitor his own performance.

It should be noted that the patient has to be able to stand up and sit down in order to practise both standing and walking. He may need assistance to stand up (see p. 105) or the therapist may need to arrange for him to have a chair of suitable height and firmness from which he is able to stand up.

The patient should spend short periods during the day standing at a table. The limb load monitor can be used to ensure that he supports some of his weight on the affected foot. Lack of practice of standing with hips forward results in shortening of the calf muscles, which will prevent him from standing with weight through his affected leg and will also interfere significantly with walking training.

### FURTHER READING

See references in Appendix 5.

# 8
# *Walking*

## DESCRIPTION OF NORMAL FUNCTION

Normal walking in an adult involves a movement of the centre of gravity through space in such a way as to require the least possible expenditure of energy.[1] It requires little muscle activity and is rhythmical and symmetrical in nature. Adults walking normally take approximately 100 steps per minute.[2] Walking is a complex function and, although there have been many biomechanical and electromyographical studies,[3-5] there is as yet no complete picture of what is involved. Several gait laboratories are attempting to establish normative data.

Biped level walking is a very unstable movement. Perturbations result from the large gravitational and forward momentum forces acting while the body is supported on one limb for 80% of the time. This is inherently unstable and requires complex control.[3]

Electromyographical studies indicate that, during the walking cycle, muscles act only over brief periods,[3,6,7] the limbs being carried forward to a large extent by their own momentum. Muscular activity is said to be involved more in deceleration than in actual progression. For example, the major action of the pretibial extensor group does not occur to lift the foot but at a point immediately after heel contact to decelerate the foot.[2,6] Gluteus maximus acts briefly following heel contact, then again at the end of the stance phase. The hamstrings contract and reach a peak of activity just after heel strike, and then again at the end of stance phase. The quadriceps also show their major activity before and at heel strike to decelerate the leg and then to absorb the impact by allowing a controlled flexion just after heel strike. Rectus femoris acts to control the pre-swing phase yield of the knee.[7]

Energy storage and recovery are efficient in normal walking because of the precise relationship between muscle contraction and displacement of body and limb segments and the brief periods during which muscles are active.[6] These factors also ensure that walking is rhythmical, with a natural cadence.

**Neural Control of Locomotion.** The way in which locomotion is achieved by the central nervous system has been a subject of study for many years. Although increased understanding of neural mechanisms controlling locomotion has come almost exclusively from experiments on animals, this knowledge may be of significance in increasing our understanding of human locomotion.

Mott and Sherrington observed after sectioning dorsal roots in a monkey that the animal would not use the affected limbs for normal walking. These observations suggested that peripheral feedback was required for normal walking and this gave rise to the notion that locomotion might be accomplished by set of 'chain reflexes' in which the sensory input from a given part of a step cycle would trigger the next part of the cycle by reflex action. However, in 1911, Graham Brown found that sectioning of the spinal cord in cats triggered rhythmic walking movements that persisted for a minute or so following the sectioning, even in animals whose dorsal roots had been previously severed bilaterally. It appears, therefore, that walking movements are not reflex in origin but are generated by neurons located in the spinal cord.[8]

Brown proposed that although afferent input is not essential for the fundamental motor pattern it is probably important to modulate walking in order to compensate for changes in the environment. This viewpoint is still considered to be essentially correct; centrally located sets of neurons (called central pattern generators or neural oscillators), which can be modulated by descending control from supraspinal brain structures, produce a rhythmic output without the necessity for afferent feedback. Afferent input, however, provides modulation of the programme according to the needs posed by a change in the environment.

For the purposes of description, walking can be divided into stance (support) phase and swing phase (Fig. 8.1), although there is also a brief period of double support.

### Stance Phase

This phase, which begins with heel strike, is characterised by plantarflexion then dorsiflexion of the ankle; flexion of the knee (the 'yield' of the

**Fig. 8.1** *The normal sequence of walking.*

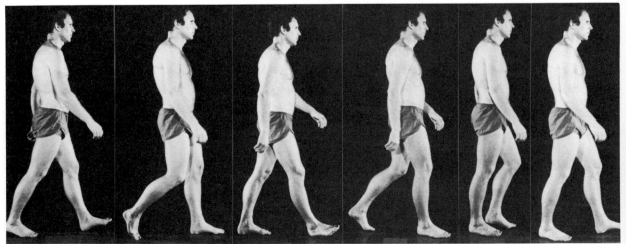

knee) which is followed by extension, with flexion occurring at the end of the phase; and extension of the hip which is continuous throughout the phase. These components enable the centre of gravity to be translated forward. Extension of the hip at the end of the stance phase appears to be essential for the initiation of the swing phase of that leg, allowing the switch to be made from one phase to the other.[9] The flexion–extension–flexion of the knee gives walking its smoothness. As weight is shifted forward and laterally, the pelvis is prevented from dropping down or 'listing' on the opposite side more than the normal few degrees by contraction of the hip abductors of the supporting leg and the trunk lateral flexors of the non-weight-bearing side (Fig. 8.2). That is, the hip joint of the swing leg is never elevated to the extent of the hip of the stance leg. The knee of the swing leg must therefore continue its flexion in order to 'shorten' the leg and enable it to swing through.[6] The contraction of the hip abductors of the standing leg also serves to control the amount of pelvic shift sideways, which is minimal and only as much as is necessary to shift the centre of gravity sufficiently laterally to allow the opposite leg to swing through. Excessive lateral displacement of the centre of gravity is also corrected by the presence of the tibio-femoral angle; that is, the abduction of the tibia relative to the femur which occurs when the knee is extended and the femur is adducting at the hip.[6]

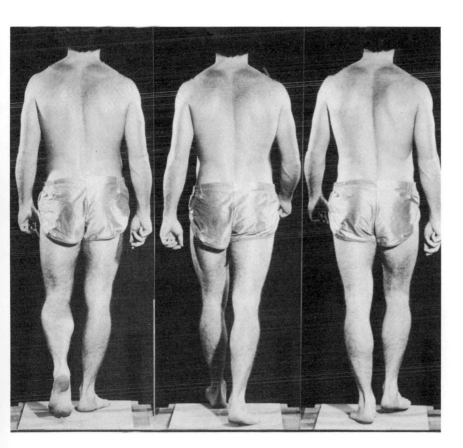

**Fig. 8.2** *Normal walking. Note (i) the very small lateral shift in the centre of gravity; (ii) the narrow base of support; (iii) the head and trunk adjustments to the lateral shifts.*

## Swing Phase

Early flexion of the knee at the beginning of swing phase decreases the moment of inertia of the lower limb, which in turn decreases the amount of hip flexor activity required.[1] The knee has virtually completed its flexion motion by the time the hip flexes and this combined hip and knee flexion shortens the leg and allows the swing foot to clear the ground following toe-off. The early swing phase is thus characterised by hip flexion, the completion of knee flexion and dorsiflexion of the ankle. The final period consists of knee extension prior to heel strike, and ankle dorsiflexion which terminates immediately following heel strike.

The shift of the centre of gravity forward is accomplished by a shift of the body weight as a whole forward by movement at the ankle and hip. The stability of the body throughout walking is related to the width of the base of support. Although a position with feet a few inches apart is normal in standing, this foot position would involve an excessive lateral horizontal shift of the pelvis if carried through to walking. Instead, the feet move directly forward from a position close together (Fig. 8.2). This limits the amount of lateral shift to a minimum while at the same time giving stability. The shift in centre of gravity necessitates compensatory adjustments within the trunk and neck in order to preserve balance. This requirement is minimised during average walking, but becomes more necessary if speed is decreased. Walking too slowly not only requires more balance but it also causes variations in the person's usual walking pattern. Less postural adjustment is involved in fast walking.

In normal walking, rotation of the pelvis occurs in a horizontal plane, but the magnitude of this rotation is small (4° on either side of the central axis),[1] its maximum excursion occurring at heel strike. This pelvic rotation is counteracted by thoracic rotation. In their study, Murray *et al.*[10] found an absence of pelvic rotation in some of their subjects, and a significant positive correlation between stride length and rotation. Although

**Fig. 8.3** *Normal walking. Some of the essential components.*

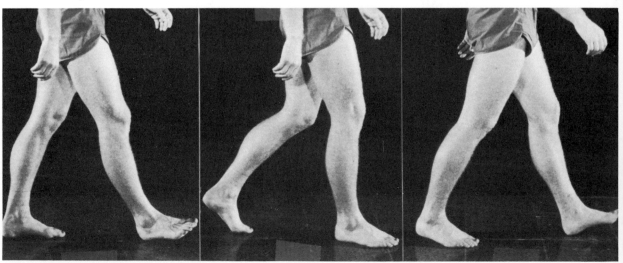

Saunders *et al.*[1] listed pelvic rotation as a major determinant of walking, Murray and his co-workers suggest that pelvic and thoracic rotation may not be essential components of smooth walking.

Since the pelvis is a rigid structure, rotation takes place at the hip joints and in the joints of the spine. The hip joint rotates internally during its swing phase until the position of full weight-bearing during stance phase is achieved, when there is a reversal into external rotation.[6]

Sagittal rotation (anterior and posterior pelvic tilting) occurs through a mean excursion of 3°, with maximum anterior tilt occurring just before heel strike and maximum posterior tilt early in stance phase.[10]

Arm swing during walking is relaxed and counteracts the tendency of the trunk to rotate away from the supporting leg. For example, as the right leg swings forward, the pelvis tends to rotate towards the left side. This is counteracted by a forward movement of the left shoulder with an associated arm swing.

ESSENTIAL COMPONENTS OF WALKING (Figs. 8.1 to 8.3)

**Stance Phase**

- Extension of the hip throughout (angular displacement taking place at ankle as well as hip).

- Lateral horizontal shift of the pelvis and trunk (normally approximately 4–5 cm (1.5–2 in) in total.

- Flexion of the knee (approximately 15°) initiated on heel strike, followed by extension, then flexion prior to toe-off.

**Swing Phase**

- Flexion of the knee, with the hip initially in extension.

- Lateral pelvic tilt downwards (approximately 5°) in the horizontal plane at toe-off.

- Flexion of the hip.

- Rotation of the pelvis forward on the swinging leg (3–4° on either side of the central axis depending on stride length).*

- Extension of the knee plus dorsiflexion of the ankle immediately prior to heel strike.

The above components are the major determinants or biomechanical necessities of walking.

---

* This does not need to be specifically trained as it will occur once hip extension and knee control during stance phase and knee flexion during swing phase have been trained.

## Walking Backwards

Weight is not shifted backwards *during* swing phase in the same manner as it is shifted in walking forward. A new base is provided *before* weight is shifted because of the inherent instability of the activity. During swing phase, the hip and knee flex, then the hip extends a short distance with the knee held in flexion (Fig. 8.4) until the toes touch the ground. Only then is weight shifted backwards, with further extension of the supporting hip and extension of the knee. Walking backwards is slower than walking forward, there are fewer visual cues and step length is shorter. Electromyographical studies indicate that muscles are more active than in forward walking,[11] which may be due to the relative lack of momentum in carrying the leg backwards.

## Walking Up and Down Stairs

Walking up and down stairs is described in detail by Andriacchi and his co-workers.[12]

Walking up stairs involves similar movement components to level walking, but the ranges of movement at the joints involved and muscle activity required are different in some respects. For example, a larger range of hip and knee flexion is required. When the foot is placed on the step, there is a forward inclination of the body at the supporting ankle and a forward and upwards shift in the centre of gravity over the forward leg (Fig. 8.5a).

**Fig. 8.4** *Walking backwards. The L. knee is held in flexion while the hip is extending.*

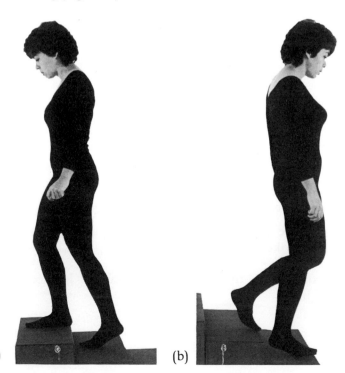

**Fig. 8.5a** *Walking up stairs.*

**Fig. 8.5b** *Walking down stairs.*    (a)          (b)

Walking down stairs has safety as its major consideration. Therefore, unlike both walking and walking up stairs, the centre of gravity is kept back over the supporting leg. The movement is performed by a controlled eccentric (lengthening) contraction of the hip and knee extensors of the supporting leg (Fig. 8.5b).

### STEP 1    ANALYSIS OF WALKING

The major problems found on analysis will be as follows.

#### Stance Phase of Affected Leg

- Lack of extension at hip and dorsiflexion at ankles (Fig. 8.6).

- Lack of controlled knee flexion–extension from 0–15° (Fig. 8.6).

- Excessive lateral horizontal shift of pelvis (Fig. 8.7).

- Excessive downwards pelvic tilt on the intact side associated with excessive lateral pelvic shift to the affected side (Fig. 8.7).

**Fig. 8.6** *This woman holds her knee in the fully extended position throughout stance phase because she lacks control over the quadriceps from 0° to 15°. Note also the lack of both extension at the hip and dorsiflexion at the ankle.*

**Fig. 8.7** *This man has shifted his weight too far to his affected R. side. As a consequence, his pelvis has dropped down on the L. side. Note the hyperextended knee.*

Fig. 8.6                    Fig. 8.7

### Swing Phase of Affected Leg

- Lack of knee flexion at toe-off (Figs. 8.8 and 8.9).

- Lack of hip flexion.

- Lack of knee extension plus ankle dorsiflexion on heel strike (Fig. 8.10).

In addition, the patient lacks the idea of the sequencing of components and of the rhythm and timing of walking.

Walking is a particularly complex activity and analysis of problems is difficult. However, analysis of the reasons why a patient cannot walk in the first few days after his stroke will usually indicate that he is unable to perform any of the essential components, because of the lack of muscle activity. It is important at this time that the therapist analyses the patient's problems correctly and makes the correct decisions about the components upon which training should concentrate. Below are some guidelines for the therapist to follow, particularly in the early period of training.

1. **Analysis and subsequent training of walking always begin with the affected leg in stance phase.** It is essential that the patient acquire the ability to bear weight through his leg in normal alignment with hip extension, controlled knee extension and the ability to shift the centre of gravity approximately 2·5 cm (1 in) laterally to the affected

**Fig. 8.8** *Swing phase of the affected leg. Note the lack of knee flexion at toe-off which is necessary to allow the foot to clear the ground.*

**Fig. 8.9** *Note the elevation and backward tilt of the pelvis and abduction of hip in compensation for lack of knee flexion throughout the initial part of swing phase; and the wide base.*

**Fig. 8.10** *This woman lacks foot dorsiflexion for heel strike. She also lacks knee flexion critical to swing phase and hence the knee is extended too soon.*

Fig. 8.8                Fig. 8.9                Fig. 8.10

side. The patient will then be able to practise stepping forward with his intact leg, and this will position his affected leg for swing phase.

Although it may appear when the patient first stands up that his major difficulty is in initiating swing phase, it will be much easier to retrain the essential components in this phase once he has control of weight-bearing through the affected leg. There are probably several reasons for this. (a) Control of the pelvis on the leg is essential to the assumption and maintenance of a well-aligned position, as the pelvis provides a link between the supporting leg and the rest of the body. (b) Once some motor control is gained in stance phase, the muscles which are involved in the swing phase seem to be in a state of 'readiness'. That is, the hip flexors seem better able to swing the affected leg forward when this leg is positioned behind the intact leg, as the extended position of the hip initiates the pendular movement involved in swing phase. This is not the case from the standing position, when the hip flexors must work immediately against the full force of gravity. Flexion of the hip requires three times the amount of energy when knee flexion is absent[1] and hence the hesitancy seen at the start of swing phase if the patient attempts to set off with his affected leg first.

2. **Difficulty translating or shifting the centre of gravity laterally** in order to free the intact leg for swinging forward. Most patients shift their pelvis too far laterally and this results in a compensatory tilt of the pelvis downwards on the intact side (see Fig. 8.7). This excessive lateral shift is usually due to a difficulty contracting the ipsilateral hip abductors and contralateral trunk side flexors at the appropriate moment. It may result in part from lack of control over 0–15° of knee extension, as the 'locked back' knee position will affect the normal tibio femoral angle, which in turn will affect the degree of lateral pelvic shift.[6] Excessive lateral shift is also usually associated with lack of hip extension which disturbs the normal body alignment at this point of stance phase and disrupts the mechanism which normally controls lateral shift.

3. **Inability to extend the affected hip** to shift the centre of gravity forward. When they first stand up, most patients have difficulty standing with their hips in the normal extended alignment. If hip extension is not trained, the centre of gravity cannot be shifted forward normally when a step is taken with the *intact leg*, and two errors of movement occur in compensation: (a) the body is not moved forward until the intact foot is on the ground, and (b) it is thus shifted forward not by extension of the affected leg but by extension of the intact leg with the affected hip in a flexed position. When a step is taken with the *affected leg*, another error occurs in compensation. Instead of weight being moved forward on to the affected leg by extension at the hip, the patient flexes his trunk forward on his affected hip and takes a short step forward with his intact leg.

Lack of hip extension, by affecting normal alignment, also makes impossible the control of the knee through the 0–15° necessary during stance phase, and causes the patient to shift his weight too far laterally. Extension of the hip may be prevented by short calf muscles which prevent the translation of the body forward (which requires angular displacement at ankle as well as hip).

4. **Lack of knee control** throughout stance phase. When the patient first takes weight through his affected leg, the knee usually collapses into flexion because of a lack of control over the knee extensors in their inner range. He will soon learn to compensate by passively levering his knee into its fully extended position and keeping it there until the end of stance phase (see Fig. 8.6). This distorts the normally smooth progression of walking brought about by the 'yield' of the knee and prevents the patient from flexing his knee prior to the start of swing phase. The problem results from an inability to contract the quadriceps and control knee extension and flexion through 0–15°. It is associated with inability to extend the hip. Many patients develop short calf muscles and this prevents hip extension and shift of the centre of gravity forward at the ankle. The knee will be kept in a stiffly extended position. Some patients learn to walk by holding the knee in slight flexion during the stance phase. This indicates that the patient does have the muscle activity to hold his knee in a slightly flexed position but insufficient control of the last few degrees of movement.

Control over the knee during stance is very complex, requiring first an eccentric or lengthening contraction of the quadriceps, then a concentric contraction to extend the knee just prior to knee flexion. Knee control must therefore be trained specifically with this complex function in mind.

5. **Lack of knee flexion at toe-off** (see Fig. 8.8) is a major problem which, due to the patient's attempts at compensation, distorts the entire sequence of swing phase. Normally, knee flexion occurs at the end of stance phase while the hip is in an extended position. This action decreases the moment of inertia of the lower extremity. Inability to flex the knee at this point produces in compensation an abnormal swing forward of the affected leg, which involves hitching of the pelvis, abduction of the hip and backward tilting of the pelvis. In analysing this phase, it may appear that lack of hip flexion is the major problem. However, although the patient may indeed lack a few degrees of flexion at the hip, once he has gained sufficient active knee flexion to allow his foot to clear the ground, hip flexion will usually be seen to be quite sufficient for walking. Hip flexion may need to be trained at some stage in rehabilitation in order that the patient can gain sufficient hip movement to step over objects and walk up stairs.

6. **Lack of active dorsiflexion** at the end of swing phase should not be considered as a problem to be treated in isolation. The major activity in the dorsiflexors normally occurs in stance phase just after heel strike and, although they are active before this, it is the flexion of the knee which 'shortens' the leg and allows the foot to clear the ground at the start of swing phase. Hence, if the patient drags his foot during swing phase, the major missing component to be trained will be knee flexion. Lack of dorsiflexion on heel strike is trained specifically in combination with the knee extension which normally accompanies it.

7. **A wide base** during practice of stepping forward or walking occurs principally due to poor balance and a fear of falling and will, therefore, be overcome by balance training with the feet closer together, that is, under the hips. However, in the early stages, it may also be due to the patient's inability to control the affected leg during swing phase (see Fig. 8.9). The compensatory movements which occur due to inability to flex the knee at toe-off may result in the affected foot being placed in a relatively abducted position. In addition, in stance phase, the poor alignment which results from lack of hip extension and excessive lateral horizontal shift towards the affected side may result in the intact foot stepping out to the side.

NOTE

If the walking section of this Programme is to be effective, it is essential that the analysis of problems is accurate and that the correct decisions are made as to the most essential components to be trained (which should be those components upon which many other components depend), and the sequence in which they are trained. For example, the patient may lack rotation of his pelvis forward on the affected side during stance. This, however, is part of the synergy of hip extension and it is this component that should be trained. The use of resistance to walking in an attempt to promote rotation will distort the walking action by interfering with or preventing hip extension throughout stance phase. Walking against resistance is not indicated for stroke patients as it interferes with both spatial and temporal aspects of the functional synergy, encourages incorrect muscle activity and interferes with the complex learning process.

To learn to walk again the stroke patient must have some muscle activity on his affected side as well as the opportunity to practise walking. It is only by observing his attempts to walk that the therapist can analyse the muscle–joint components as they occur. One cannot infer the presence or absence of muscle action required in walking from clinical tests such as manual muscle strength tests or the response to stretch.

## STEP 2    PRACTICE OF MISSING COMPONENTS

### Stance Phase

**To Train Hip Extension Throughout Stance Phase**

See p. 116 for eliciting activity in hip extensors.

*Standing with hip in correct alignment, patient practises stepping forward then backwards with intact leg, making sure he extends his affected hip as he steps forward.*

NOTE

This should not be done too slowly nor should step size be too big. It is to give the patient the idea of standing on his affected leg while moving his intact leg. It can be followed by having the patient shift weight on to the intact leg so he can start to walk.

INSTRUCTIONS
'Take your weight through your (affected) leg.'
'Step forward with this (intact) leg. You need to move forward at your (affected) ankle.'

CHECK
Make sure patient does not step out to the side. Indicate where he is to step.
Make sure hip extends throughout.
Make sure hips do not move more than 2 cm laterally on stance leg.

### To Train Knee Control for Stance Phase

*Sitting (supine if hamstrings are tight), with knee held straight, therapist gives firm pressure through heel towards knee while patient (i) practises controlling an eccentric and concentric contraction of the quadriceps through a 15° range (Fig. 8.11), and (ii) attempts to keep knee straight (isometric contraction). Pressure through the heel must be as firm as possible so the quadriceps must contract to prevent the knee from flexing.*

NOTE
It may be easier for the patient to activate his knee extensors (to keep his knee from bending further) with his knee held at 15° or 20° first, then to straighten it further a few degrees, bend it again, and so on until he is practising in the required 0–15° range. It is critical that the quadriceps can be activated. See p. 118 for other ways of eliciting and training activity in these muscles.

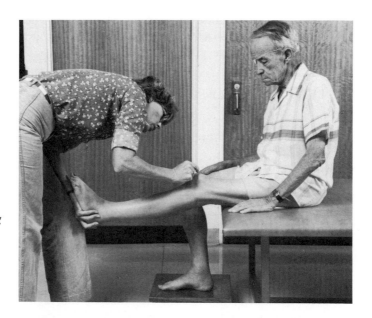

**Fig. 8.11** *Patient practises flexing and extending his knee through 0–15° to improve control over his quadriceps in this range. Pressure through his heel ensures that the activity in the quadriceps is eccentric when he bends his knee.*

INSTRUCTIONS
(i) 'Bend your knee a little—not too much. Now straighten it.'
(ii) 'Keep your knee straight.'

CHECK
Make sure the patient's leg is positioned so that the bed does not block full knee extension and to allow hip as well as knee movement. It is the thigh that moves on the lower leg, not the lower leg on the thigh.
Do not allow knee movement to become jerky or uncontrolled.
(i)  The patient should practise in the part of the range he can just control, progressing to moving in the 0–15° range as soon as possible.
(ii)  As soon as he has some control, he practises holding his knee at varying positions between 0° and 15°.
In (ii) the knee must not be 'locked' into extension.
Do not allow him to plantarflex his foot.

Followed by:

*Patient stands up and practises stepping forward and backwards with intact leg as above.*

*Standing with intact leg in front of affected leg (Fig. 8.12). Patient practises moving his weight forward over his intact foot and back while maintaining*

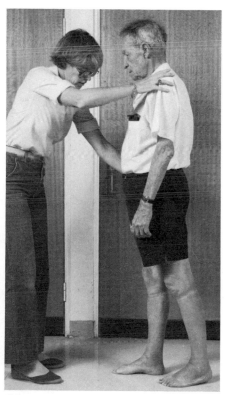

(a)                    (b)

Fig. 8.12 (a) *This man's affected L. knee has flexed before his weight is sufficiently forward.* (b) *He shifts his weight forward and practises bending and straightening his L. knee.*

*knee extension of the affected leg. The step size should be small or it will be inappropriate to keep the knee extended. The patient may get a better idea of how to control his knee if he flexes his knee a few degrees then extends it. Weight must be forward over the intact leg as he practises this, so he is practising controlling his knee with little weight through the leg.*

INSTRUCTIONS
'Move your hips forward over your (intact) foot.'
'Keep your knees straight.'
'Practise bending and straightening your (affected) knee a few degrees. Keep your hip forward while you do this.'

CHECK
Make sure affected knee remains straight—as the patient moves forward it may tend to flex.

The following will add variety to practice and further train knee control.

*Patient steps on and off an 8 cm (3 in) step with intact foot.*

INSTRUCTIONS
'Put your (intact) foot on to the step.'
'Keep your (affected) hip straight.'
'Put your foot back down again.'

CHECK
Ensure that centre of gravity is not shifted backwards as patient places intact foot on step, i.e. affected hip must be extended throughout.
Do not allow affected knee to flex or hyperextend.
Do not allow him to step out to the side.

*Standing with affected foot on step. Patient shifts weight forward and steps up on to step and back down again with intact leg (Fig. 8.13). Progress to stepping over.*

INSTRUCTIONS
'Put this (affected) foot on to the step.'
'Move your (affected) knee forward.'
'Step up with the other (intact) leg.'
'Keep your knee bent until your weight is forward.'
'Now, straighten your knee.'

CHECK
Do not allow knee to extend prematurely, i.e. knee must not be extended until it is well in front of the ankle.
Make sure he does not push himself up with intact leg instead of lifting his weight on his affected leg.
When stepping over the step with his intact leg, he must extend his affected knee fully in mid stance.
Make sure he does not put his intact foot to the ground prematurely but lowers his foot to the ground slowly.

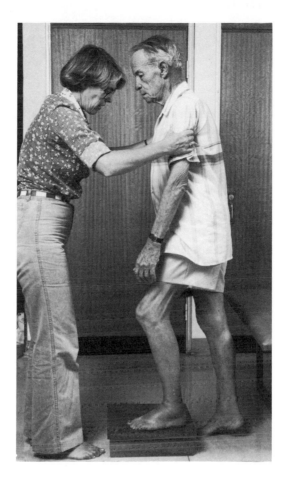

**Fig. 8.13** *This man, with the therapist's guidance, is shifting his centre of gravity forward over his affected foot, i.e. moving his L. knee forward, as he steps up with his intact R. leg. The therapist may need to guide the knee forward.*

NOTE

The above is a useful way to strengthen the quadriceps, but only if it is done repeatedly. The height of the step can be varied. It is also used to train the movements required for walking up stairs and can be followed by practice of this.

## To Train Lateral Horizontal Pelvic Shift

*In standing, hips in front of ankles, patient practises shifting his weight from one foot to the other (Fig. 8.14a). The therapist indicates with her finger how far his pelvis should shift, i.e. 2·5 cm (approximately 1 inch).*

INSTRUCTIONS

'Move your weight over on to your right foot.'
'Now move it back on to your left foot.'
'To move to the right, push down gently through your left foot.'

CHECK

Make sure hips and knees remain extended.
He must not shift his pelvis too far laterally.

*In standing, hips over feet, patient practises stepping forward with intact leg (Fig. 8.14b).*

*Walking sideways* (Fig. 8.15).

NOTE
If the patient cannot abduct his affected leg to step, therapist helps him, using her own foot to guide the step as soon as weight is shifted to the intact leg. If necessary, patient can rest his arms on the therapist's shoulders. This gives him a little support. His elbows should be extended and he should not hang on around the therapist's neck.

INSTRUCTIONS
'Let's walk sideways. Stand on your right leg and step sideways with your left foot.'
'Stand on your left leg. Now, feet together.'

CHECK
Make sure shoulders remain level.
Hips must remain in front of ankles—he must progress sideways not diagonally. Walking along a line will guide him.
He must not shift his pelvis too far laterally.

**Fig. 8.14 (a)** *This man is practising shifting his weight laterally onto his affected R. foot. Note the therapist's finger indicating the small range of movement required.* **(b)** *Here, he is about to take a step forward with the L. leg. Note that at this point he needs to extend his R. hip more. His excessive lateral shift is associated with lack of hip extension and controlled knee extension.*

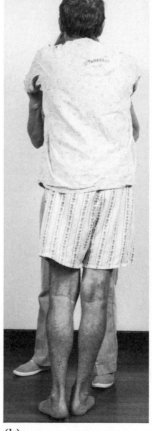

(a)                              (b)

(a)                              (b)

**Fig. 8.15 (a)** *and* **(b)** *Walking sideways. This man is taking a step to the L. Note that he has not yet gained the ability to shift his weight to the L. simultaneously with the L. hip abduction.*

## Swing Phase

### To Train Flexion of Knee at Start of Swing Phase

*To elicit activity in the knee flexors, have the patient lie prone on bed. Therapist flexes knee to just below a right-angle. Patient practises (i) controlling his knee flexors both eccentrically and concentrically throughout a small range of movement, (ii) holding his knee in different parts of the range, sustaining muscle activity to counting (Fig. 8.16).*

NOTE

With the knee at a right-angle, it is usually easier for the patient to contract the knee flexors. As the patient gains control around this point, he is encouraged to increase the range of movement. He must try actively to gain control over his hamstrings throughout their middle range. The therapist must ensure that the hip does not flex as the patient attempts to activate his knee flexors. If the patient is only able to activate them in conjunction with hip flexion and not under any other circumstance, this is not compatible with normal function. The therapist should keep in mind the effect a tight rectus femoris muscle will have on the range of knee flexion which can be achieved without the hip flexing.

**Fig. 8.16** *Patient practises controlling knee flexors.*

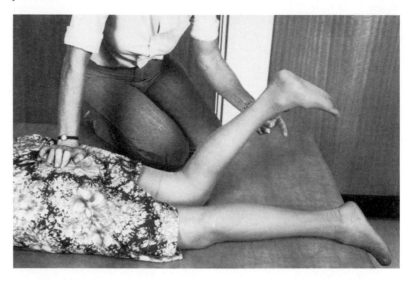

**INSTRUCTIONS**
(i) 'Hold your knee there—bend it up a little—now let it down slowly.'
'Bend it up again. Don't be jerky—make a smooth slow movement.'
'Keep your hip down.'
(ii) 'Hold your foot here for the count of . . .'
'Hold it for longer this time.'

**CHECK**
Do not allow jerky uncontrolled movement. Therapist may assist by taking some of the weight of the leg.
Do not allow the hip to flex.

Followed by :

*Standing, therapist holds patient's knee in some flexion. He practises controlled eccentric and concentric knee flexion (Fig. 8.17).*

**NOTE**
It is often easier for the patient to take his toes down to the floor (an eccentric contraction of his knee flexors) *before* lifting them up from the floor (a concentric contraction).

**INSTRUCTIONS**
'Give me your leg. Don't let your hip bend.'
'Take your toes down to touch the floor.'
'Now, lift your toes up off the floor.'

**CHECK**
Do not flex his knee too much. This will pull him off balance, and tension on his rectus femoris will cause his hip to flex as well as making it difficult for him to contract his knee flexors.
Do not allow hip to bend more than a few degrees.
Do not push the patient off balance—hold his opposite arm, and make sure his weight is balanced over his standing foot.

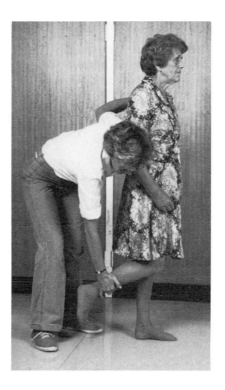

**Fig. 8.17** *Patient practises controlling knee flexion before stepping forward.*

Followed by:

*Patient steps forward with affected leg, therapist helping him control the initial knee flexion.*

**INSTRUCTIONS**
'Bend your knee.'
'Step forward. Heel down first '

**CHECK**
Make sure the patient extends the hip of his standing leg as he steps forward.

*Patient walks backwards. Therapist guides knee flexion and foot dorsiflexion (Fig. 8.18).*

**INSTRUCTIONS**
'Walk backwards.'
'Bend your knee, step back and put your toes to the ground.'

**CHECK**
Do not allow patient to incline trunk forward at hips instead of extending the hip.
He should step backwards one leg after the other in a rhythmical manner.

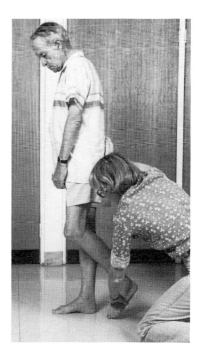

**Fig. 8.18** *Practice of walking backwards. Therapist guides the step backwards initially to give him the idea of the movement.*

### To Train Knee Extension and Foot Dorsiflexion at Heel Strike

*Patient standing on intact leg, therapist holds the patient's affected foot in dorsiflexion, with the knee in extension. Patient moves his weight forward on to heel (Fig. 8.19).*

NOTE
This technique gives the patient the idea of this component of the swing phase.

INSTRUCTIONS
'Let me have your foot. Don't hold yourself stiffly. Now, shift your weight forward so you put this heel down.'

CHECK
Do not allow him to bend the other knee. He will do this if he does not shift his weight forward by extending his hip.
Step length should be average.
Do not give too many instructions.

### STEP 3    PRACTICE OF WALKING

Practice of individual components of walking should be followed by practice of walking itself which enables the patient to put these components together in their proper sequence.

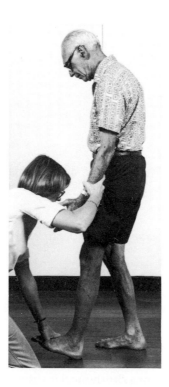

**Fig. 8.19** *At heel strike, the alignment of both lower limbs is incorrect. Weight is too far back and his R. knee is flexed. Training consists of instructing him to move forward by extending his R. hip.*

## Walking

*The patient steps with his intact leg first. The therapist steadies him at the upper arms, standing behind so as not to impede his vision and get in his way. The patient should know to stop and re-align himself when he feels 'off balance' and cannot correct this as he walks (Fig. 8.20).*

NOTE

The goal of his first few steps is for him to get the idea of the rhythm of walking, which may itself improve control and the sequencing of the components. It may be difficult for the patient to step forward with his affected leg, and the therapist, for the first few times, may need to guide his leg forward with her own. The therapist should not hold the patient too firmly as this may interfere with his performance by either offering resistance to the translation of the body mass forward or by interfering with the alignment of body segments, thus putting him off balance. Counting or saying 'right–left' or 'step–step' will help him to get the timing of the movement. The patient should walk at an average speed. Walking very slowly requires more muscle activity.

Concurrent observation and analysis of the patient's alignment as he progresses forward will enable the therapist to identify for the patient a clear goal to improve a component of his walking. For example, in stance phase, the goal may be to keep moving his hip forward so he feels the weight through the ball of his foot. At the beginning of swing phase, the goal may be to bend the knee and bring it straight forward. In other words, the goal is expressed as a strategy for overcoming a specific problem, not as the problem itself.

INSTRUCTIONS

'Now you're going to walk. Don't worry if you can't do it very well to begin with—the important thing is to get the idea of walking.'
'Step with this (intact) leg first.'

CHECK

Do not push the patient off balance.
Do not hold on to him too much.
So as not to fall over each other, when the patient steps forward with his right leg, the therapist does the same.

### To Increase Complexity

The patient needs the opportunity to improve his walking skills and he will only do this by practising walking. His new abilities must be constantly stretched to their limits, with the frequent addition to his programme of more variety. Walking in the physiotherapy area on a firm, flat surface with the therapist is practice in a very closed environment. He needs practice in an open environment with both people and objects moving. Below are some examples of increasing complexity.

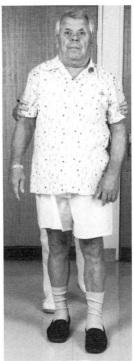

**Fig. 8.20** *Walking practice.*

*Patient practises stepping over objects of different heights.*

*Walking combined with other activities such as conversation, carrying objects.*

*Varying the speed of walking and the spatial confines within which the person walks.*

*Walking along a busy corridor.* Initially the therapist should accompany the patient to help him identify the critical environmental cues, for example intersections, doorways, traffic.

*Walking in and out of the elevator.* In this situation the patient must match his performance with the timing constraints of the closing doors.

*Treadmill walking* is another way of improving the rhythm and timing of walking. It is also a useful method of increasing cardiopulmonary efficiency and endurance and of measuring these as a guide to progress. The treadmill should be adjusted to the most comfortable speed for each person.

### STEP 4    TRANSFERENCE OF TRAINING INTO DAILY LIFE

At the end of the therapy session, the therapist allows some time for the patient to walk at least part of the way to his next appointment with

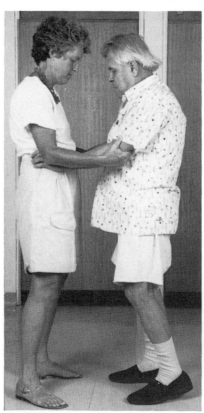

**Fig. 8.21a** *Another way to help this man walk until he can do so unaided is to steady him at his arms. Here, he is practising walking a few steps forward and a few steps backward.*

**Fig. 8.21b** *This woman needs only a little assistance and verbal instruction about the changing environmental demands. Note therapist's hand on upper arm.*

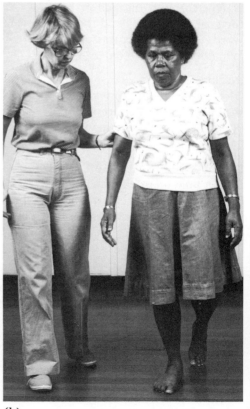

(a)    (b)

her accompanying him. He can set himself a goal of how far he walks on the first day and can extend distance and/or time taken on the next day. By measuring distance walked and time taken to cover this distance, a graph can be used to indicate improvement. As soon as possible he should walk alone.

The patient needs the opportunity to practise by himself or with other members of staff and relatives. In order to practise by himself he needs to be able to stand up and therefore needs a suitable chair. He is given written instructions so he knows what he should concentrate on. For example, these may include specific goal(s), number of repetitions, or distance to cover. He will also benefit from videotaped instructions between therapy sessions.

Figure 8.21 illustrates two ways of assisting the patient to walk. Much physiotherapy equipment traditionally used in walking rehabilitation is based on assumptions which are in direct conflict with the assumptions on which this motor learning model is based. For example, the assumptions underlying the practice of walking in parallel bars are that they provide safety and compensate for lack of balance and that walking in parallel bars will generalise into unaided walking in other more open environments. However, standing and walking aids such as parallel bars or a three-point cane will alleviate only transiently the patient's balance problems, and when used continually will worsen the problems since control mechanisms rapidly adapt to the additional feedback and support provided.[13] Some patients may, however, need a regular cane to steady them and some may have used a cane before their stroke. The therapist explains to the patient how to use the cane to steady himself rather than leaning on it. A longer than normal cane may assist this.

The use of a device to hold the foot in dorsiflexion (splint, short leg brace with ankle stops) is not advised. It holds the foot in dorsiflexion throughout the walking cycle, preventing the dorsiflexion–plantarflexion which is necessary at certain stages of the cycle. The patient will have to compensate for this restriction of angular displacement at the ankle by altering the angular displacement at hip and knee.

## REFERENCES

1. Saunders J. B., Inman V. T. and Eberhart H. D. (1953). The major determinants in normal and pathological gait. *J. Bone Jt Surg*; **35A**, 3:543–58.
2. Dubo H. I. C., Peat M., Winter D. A., Quanbury A. O., Hobson D. A., Steinke T. and Reimer G. (1976). Electromyographic temporal analysis of gait: normal human locomotion. *Arch. phys. Med*; **57**:415–20.
3. Winter D. A. (1983). Biomechanical motor patterns in normal walking. *J. Motor Behavior*; **15** (4):302–328.
4. Milner M., Basmajian J. V. and Quanbury A. O. (1971). Multifactorial analysis of walking by electromyography and computer. *Amer. J. phys. Med*; **50**:235–58.
5. Battye C. K. and Joseph J. (1966). An investigation by telemetering of the activity of some muscles in walking. *Med biol. Engng*; **4**:125–35.

6. Eberhard H. D., Inman V. T. and Bresler B. (1969). The principal elements in human locomotion. In *Human Limbs and their Substitutes* (Klopstag P. F. and Wilson D. P., eds.) pp. 437–471. New York: McGraw Hill.

7. Herman R., Cook T., Cozzens B. and Freedman W. (1973). Control of postural reactions in man: the initiation of gait. In *Control of Posture and Locomotion* (Stein R. B. *et al.*, eds.) pp. 363–388. New York: Plenum Press.

8. Kandel E. R. and Schwartz J. H. (1981). In *Principles of Neural Science*, pp. 316–332. New York: Elsevier/North Holland.

9. Pearson K. (1976). The control of walking. *Scientific American*; **December**:72–86.

10. Murray M. P., Drought A. B. and Kory R. C. (1964). Walking patterns of normal men. *J. Bone Jt Surg*; **46A,2**:335–60.

11. Kramer J. F. and Reid D. C. (1981). Backward walking: a cinematographic and electromyographic pilot study. *Physiotherapy Canada*; **33,2**:77–86.

12. Andriacchi T. P., Andersson G. B. J., Fermier R. W., Stern D. and Galante J. O. (1980). A study of lower limb mechanics during stair-climbing. *J. Bone Jt Surg*; **62A**:749–57.

13. Brandt T., Krafczyk S. and Malsbender I. (1981). Postural imbalance with head extension: improvement by training as a model for ataxia therapy. *Ann. N.Y. Acad. Sci*; 636–649.

## FURTHER READING

Aptekar R. G., Ford F. and Bleck E. E. (1976). Light patterns as a means of assessing and recording gait: methods and results in normal children. *Develop. Med. Child Neurol*; **18**:31–6.

Carlsöös S. (1966). The initiation of walking. *Acta anat*; **65**:1–9.

Gronley J. K., and Perry J. (1984). Gait analysis techniques. *Phys. Ther*; **64**:1831–1838.

Holt K. S., Jones R. B. and Wilson R. (1974). Gait analysis by means of a multiple sequential exposure camera. *Develop. Med. Child Neurol*; **16**:742–5.

Inman V. T. (1947). Functional aspects of the abductor muscles of the hip. *J. Bone Jt Surg*; **29**:607–19.

Murray M. P., Drought A. B. and Kory R. C. (1969). Walking patterns in healthy old men. *J. Geront*; **24**:169–78.

Robinson J. L. and Smidt G. L. (1981). Quantitative gait evaluation in the clinic. *Arch. Phys. Med*; **61**:351–3.

Van Ingen Schenau G. J. (1980). Some fundamental aspects of the biomechanics of overground versus treadmill locomotion. *Medicine and Science in Sports and Exercise*; **12**:257–61.

Winter D. A. (1981). Use of kinetic analysis in the diagnostics of pathological gait. *Physiotherapy Canada*; **3**:209–30.

# PART III

Appendices

# Appendix 1

# Mechanisms of recovery

Although little is actually known of what occurs in the human brain following damage to its structure, it is probable that recovery can occur as a result of changes in neural organisation which take place in response to injury. A number of hypothetical considerations of adaptation and reorganisation are to be found in the literature.[1-11] Anatomical evidence supports the notion that new central connections are formed.[12-14] Certainly, the often impressive degree of recovery of function seen in adults following even apparently extensive lesions of the brain suggests that changes are occurring within the nervous system.

Some of the theories and mechanisms which have been proposed to account for recovery following brain damage are as follows.

1. **von Monakow's diaschisis theory.** This is a theory of a temporary traumatic disruption of neural organisation and integration, which is a type of 'functional shock'.[15] This theory suggests that the widespread effects of such processes as oedema and extracellular blood flow cause a suppression of activity in areas far from the site of the lesion. Similarly, reversible changes may occur in undamaged synapses resulting in a temporary impairment of neural transmission. This theory could account for any recovery of function in the early period following a lesion.

2. Another theory which may provide part of the explanation for early recovery is that of **denervation supersensitivity**. The axons and terminals degenerate following a lesion and the denervated part of the target cells may develop an increased post-synaptic responsiveness to neurotransmitter substances, becoming increasingly sensitive to the remaining afferent input.[9]

3. **Redundancy theory.**[16] Several parts of the central nervous system may mediate the same motor function. That is, a part of a neural system may adequately mediate the function normally subserved by the system as a whole. Lashley[17] had a similar concept which he called equipotentiality. He suggested that a particular function was mediated by all the tissues in a given region. If part of that region was damaged, the remaining intact tissue would continue to mediate that function. The effect of the lesion would therefore depend more on the **amount** of tissue spared than on the **location** of the lesion.

4. **Vicarious function.** The intact system may have had a latent capacity to control the functions which are lost. After a lesion these latent functions would become overt.[9]

5. **Functional reorganisation.** It is possible that a neural system can change its functions qualitatively, in which case a neural pathway could take over the control of some motor behaviour not ordinarily part of its repertoire.[9]

6. Two forms of **neural sprouting** within the central nervous system have been suggested. (a) **Regeneration,** which refers to new growth in damaged neurons. The newly generated axons may re-innervate the denervated areas. (b) **Collateral sprouting,** in which there is new growth in undamaged neurons adjacent to destroyed neural tissue. Sprouting would increase synaptic effectiveness and allow the new system to substitute for the destroyed synapses. The emergence of new synaptic connections may be indicative of a dynamic synaptogenesis which is continually occurring under normal circumstances,[12] enabling the organism to adjust in the face of continually changing environmental needs. These widespread synaptic changes may be the underlying physiological mechanism for a relearning or compensatory process which is actually responsible for recovery and is no more fundamental than the changes which occur in any learning situation.[18] Laurence and Stein[15] suggest that it is possible that in the normal brain 'cells may die leaving a number of vacated sites which can be filled by intact cells. In this way, the mature brain may differ from the immature one by virtue of the greater number and complexity of its interneural connections and elaboration made at the expense of absolute cell numbers'.[15]

7. **Behavioural strategy change.** This is a form of **substitution,** in which the strategy utilised in order to achieve a motor goal is different. Other forms of substitution may involve the use of a different sensory cue for guiding movement, or a functional substitution in which the recovered movements are produced differently from the lost movements, although they are essentially the same.[19] Certainly, one of the problems in research in this area is the difficulty in identifying whether recovery is due to anatomical and physiological changes or to the use of alternative or compensatory strategies by the subject.

Other theories suggest that previously ineffective synapses may become effective following disruption of input to nerve cells, and that there may be spontaneous changes in inhibitory activity. This process may explain in part the recovery from the stage of depressed motor activity or 'cerebral shock'. Chemical changes may occur which enhance the process of synaptic modification.[10] Studies carried out by Goldberger[9] indicate that motor recovery after a lesion may not be a diffuse process but a process which is regulated hierarchically.

Assuming that the brain is capable of adaptation and reorganisation, what happens to the patient following stroke must be exceedingly important. Luria[19] suggests that an essential condition of such reorganisation is that a particular activity practised be necessary and he states that the greater the need, the more automatically and easily will reorganisation be carried out. Singer[20] comments that '. . . if certain patterns of movement have been established before injury or disease occurs, there is a better chance neurons in surrounding areas will be able to compensate for their loss of function'. Just as it can be assumed that early practice of relevant motor tasks takes advantage of the brain's plasticity, so it is also possible that lack of relevant practice can allow secondary neuronal atrophy to occur[4,14] or inappropriate neuronal synapses to be made.

Whether or not motor training stimulates anatomical and physiological reorganisation or whether it enables the patient to take advantage of it is, of course, open to question. The authors' clinical experience suggests that patients on this specific programme of motor learning, which should commence within the first few days following stroke, make a more impressive recovery of function with less reflex hyperactivity than patients receiving more 'traditional' physiotherapy. This may be due to the emphasis both on very early training of context-specific control of muscles of the affected limbs, and prevention of muscular contractures and length-associated changes, as well as on elimination of overuse of the intact side and of unnecessary muscle activity of the affected side.

Two other factors which may exert a profound influence upon recovery are the quality of the brain before the lesion occurred, and the quality of the environment in which the patient finds himself following his stroke.[21-24] Animal experiments have shown that both training[25] and the environment[26,27] have an effect upon brain structure. Bennett[28] found that the cerebral cortices of rats which spent their time in a rich and complex environment were measurably thicker and heavier than those of other rats. Furthermore, this situation could be reversed if the rats were placed in a relatively impoverished environment, indicating, according to the experimenter, that the richer environment may have provided more opportunity for learning.

## REFERENCES

1. Raisman G. (1969). Neuronal plasticity in the septal nuclei of the adult rat. *Brain Res*; **14**:15–48.
2. Wall P. D. and Egger M. D. (1971). Formation of new connexions in the adult rat brains after partial deafferentation. *Nature*; **232**:542–545.
3. Brodal A. (1973). Self-observations and neuro-anatomical considerations after a stroke. *Brain*; **96** (Part IV):675–694.
4. Eccles J. C. (1973). *The Understanding of the Brain*. New York: McGraw Hill.
5. Stein D. G., Rosen J. J. and Butters N., eds. (1974). *Plasticity and Recovery of Function in the Central Nervous System*. New York: Academic Press.
6. Goldman P. S. (1974). An alternative to developmental plasticity: heterology of CNS structures in infants and adults. In *Plasticity and Recovery of Function in the Central Nervous System* (Stein D. G., Rosen J. J. and Butters N., eds.) pp. 149–174. New York: Academic Press.
7. Finger S. (1978). *Recovery from Brain Damage*. London: Plenum Press.
8. Székely G. (1979). Order and plasticity in the nervous system. *Trends in Neuroscience*; **2**:245–8.

9. Goldberger M. (1980). Motor recovery after lesions. *Trends in Neuroscience*; **3**:288–91.

10. Kasamatsu T., Pettigrew J. D. and Ary M. (1981). Cortical recovery from effects of monocular deprivation: acceleration with Norepinephrine and suppression with 6-Hydroxydopamine. *J. Physiol*;**45**:1.

11. Miles F. A. and Lisberger S. G. (1981). Plasticity in the vestibulo-ocular reflex: a new hypothesis. *Ann. Rev. Neurosc*; **4**:273–299.

12. Chambers W. W., Liu C. N. and McCouch G. P. (1973). Anatomical and physiological correlates of plasticity in the central nervous system. *Brain, Behaviour and Evolutions*; **8**:5–26.

13. Kerr F. W. L. (1975). Structural and functional evidence for plasticity in the central nervous system. *Exp. Neur*; **48**:16–31.

14. Woolsey T. A. (1978). Lesion experiments: some anatomical considerations. In *Recovery from Brain Damage* (Finger S., ed.) pp. 71–89. London: Plenum Press.

15. Laurence S. and Stein D. G. (1978). Recovery after brain damage and the concept of localisation of function. In *Recovery from Brain Damage* (Finger S., ed.) pp. 369–407. London: Plenum Press.

16. Rosner B. S. (1970). Brain functions. *Ann. Rev. Psych*; **21**:555–594.

17. Lashley K. S. (1979). *Brain Mechanisms and Intelligence*. Chicago: University of Chicago Press.

18. Bliss T. V. P. (1979). Synaptic plasticity in the hippocampus. *Trends in Neuroscience*; **2**:42–45.

19. Luria A. R. (1963). *Restoration of Function after Brain Injury*. London: Pergamon.

20. Singer R. N. (1980). *Motor Learning and Human Performance,* 3rd edn. New York: Macmillan.

21. Rosenzweig M. R., Bennett E. L. and Diamond M. C. (1967). Effects of differential environments on brain anatomy and brain chemistry. *Proc. Amer. psychopath. Ass*; **56**:45–6.

22. Goldman P. S. (1976). The role of experience in recovery of function following orbital prefrontal lesion in infant monkeys. *Neuropsychologia*; **14**:401–12.

23. Rosenzweig M. R. and Bennett E. L. (1978). Experimental influences on brain anatomy and brain chemistry in rodents. In *Studies on the Development of Behaviour and the Nervous System* (Gottlieb G., ed.) pp.289–327. New York: Academic Press.

24. Walsh R. (1981). Sensory environments, brain damage, and drugs: a review of the interactions and mediating mechanisms. *Int. J. Neuroscience*; **14**:129–37.

25. Greenough W. (1980). Development and memory: the synaptic connection. In *Brain and Learning* (Teyler T., ed), pp.127–45. Dordrecht, Holland: Reidel.

26. Walsh R. and Greenough W. (1976). *Environments as Therapy for Brain Dysfunction*. New York: Plenum Press.

27. Lynch G. and Wells J. (1980). Neuroanatomical plasticity and behavioural adaptability. In *Brain and Learning* (Teyler T., ed), pp. 105–26. Dordrecht, Holland: Reidel.

28. Bennett E. L. (1976). Cerebral effects of differential experience and training. In *Neural Mechanisms of Learning and Memory* (Rosenzweig M. R. and Bennett E. L., eds.), pp.279–88. Cambridge, Mass: M. I. T. Press.

# Appendix 2

# *Elimination of unnecessary muscle activity*

In the very early stages following stroke, the patient demonstrates an inability to move (that is, to activate muscles) on the affected side. This depression of motor function[1] is referred to as transient flaccidity or hypotonia, although the terms paralysis and weakness are also used.

Gradually there is a return of muscle activity. From the moment activity can first be elicited, there is a tendency for the patient to make several types of error and these errors are augmented by the effort he uses as he tries hard to accomplish the desired activity.

- He may tend to activate the incorrect muscle for a particular motor task.
- He may make too strong a muscle contraction for the needs of the movement in compensation for poor control.
- He may move the intact side instead of the affected side.
- He may activate correct muscles but the dynamic relationship (spatial and temporal) between the muscles is disturbed.

His attempts to move have, therefore, the opposite to the desired effect, making the required activity even harder to accomplish.

The authors' clinical experience with stroke patients suggests that the degree of stereotyped and excessive motor activity demonstrated by a patient and the amount of motor control he is able to regain may depend as much on his experience following the stroke as upon the brain damage itself. These experiences include the patient's own attempts to move, the way in which he is assisted to move by relatives and staff, his environment, the type of physiotherapy he receives and the amount of time he spends in practice. It is probable that the abnormal synergies reported in the stroke patient may have a positional component and be related to soft tissue contracture.[2] For example, a person who is left in the sitting position tends to develop flexor overactivity and contracture in the lower limb; a person who stands early without bearing weight through the affected leg tends to develop overactivity in the quadriceps and calf muscles in this leg. The muscles which tend to become overactive and/or contracted seem to be the muscles which are held in a shortened position.

Hence, the development of muscle imbalance may, to some extent, be dependent upon certain muscles being in a better 'position' to become active with certain other muscles (their antagonists) tending *not* to be so active because of their relative disadvantage.

It is probable that the patient's experiences after stroke, occurring in conjunction with reorganisation of the brain, affect recovery, either positively, by actually stimulating reorganisation itself or by enabling the patient to take advantage of it, or negatively, by retarding or interfering with reorganisation. That is, the patient's experiences, if they are positive, will enable a learning process to take place which may itself be an important factor in the brain's reorganisation. Therefore, whether or not he learns to move efficiently will depend on the training he receives. Practice of inappropriate muscle activity will result in that activity being learned, and in a sense slowly developing spasticity is made up of habitual, incorrect and unnecessary motor responses.

The re-emergence of motor activity in individual muscles is therefore a crucial event in terms of the patient's eventual recovery of function. At this time, the physiotherapist should be training the muscle activity necessary for specific tasks and ensuring that there is not an unbalanced recovery of activity in muscles which do not normally function together. The direction which recovery of muscle activity following stroke takes— that is, into abnormal synergies or into normal functional synergies— probably depends to a large extent upon physiotherapy at this stage.

Many authors[3–5] stress the importance of motor learning consisting as much of inhibition of unnecessary activity as of activation of more units. Broer and Zernicke[6] comment that muscular control involves the ability to relax, i.e. the ability to prevent muscles which do not contribute to the maintenance of the position or the execution of the movement from contracting. They suggest that the ability to relax is as much a motor skill as any movement. Blomfield and Marr[7] suggest that movements are learned by the turning off of incorrect elemental movements, and Mac-Conaill and Basmajian[8] that expenditure of energy should be the minimum necessary to allow the desired activity to be achieved.

Kottke and co-workers[9] comment that motor patterns 'involve inhibition of neuronal pathways which should not be participating in the pattern, as well as excitation of the internuncial neurons leading to all the anterior horn cells needed in the pattern', and they go on to say that inhibition of undesired activity is more difficult than initiation of the desired activity. 'Trained inhibition', as they call it, prevents overflow of activity to other motor units and they caution that effort 'must be kept low during learning to avoid irradiation of excitation across the CNS'. The antagonist normally relaxes during a trained movement.[10] Failure to do so indicates lack of skill but it also indicates lack of motor control in the brain-damaged person.

Taub and Berman[11] point out that rehabilitation therapy could be described as additive in nature, depending on the belief that recovery of function can be achieved solely through the re-education or exercise of inactivated muscle groups. Their research with animals suggests that at least some motor deficits are caused 'not by the loss of nervous tissue as such, but rather by the unrestrained hyperactivity of certain neural centres, resulting in a disabling imbalance'.

**Overflow.** In the intact person, an overflow of activity into muscles not necessary for the task is an indication of lack of motor skill. Overflow is seen in the normal child as an indication of his motor immaturity and in the normal adult who is learning a novel motor task. Overflow is called by various terms in the physiotherapy literature, including synkinetic movements, associated movements and associated reactions.[12-14] In the brain-damaged person, however, this irradiation of muscle activity on the affected side occurs selectively in those muscles capable of strongest activation. It augments the tendency towards excessive and inappropriate motor activity and imposes upon the patient the necessity for movement to be stereotyped, certain muscles always contracting in conjunction with certain other muscles in synergic relationships unrelated to the desired motor task.

In the early stages following stroke, this abnormal motor activity may be obvious as the patient attempts to move and is probably due to the effects of muscle shortening. For example, when he attempts to grasp an object, the initial extension, which is necessary to position the fingers correctly, may be possible only if the wrist flexes since this position, by taking the stretch off the long finger flexors, allows the fingers to extend. In other patients the fingers may flex before the object is in the hand, and there will also be an overflow of muscular activity into the wrist flexors, thumb adductors and forearm pronators. These events make effective hand use impossible. It is important at this stage that both the therapist and the patient understand what is happening. They may both be delighted at the sight of some recovery of movement, and the patient may want to practise this abnormal activity. The therapist must explain to him that uncontrolled and generalised flexor activity will actually *prevent* him from regaining effective use of his hand, and she should work with him to lengthen his shortened muscles and establish control over the particular muscles needed for certain activities. Emphasis in training will be on certain important movement components (extension and radial deviation of the wrist, extension of the carpo-metacarpal joints with fingers slightly flexed, thumb abduction, forearm supination) and on helping the patient to prevent his every attempt at movement from being directed solely into his flexors, ulnar deviators and pronators.

Although overflow of muscle activity tends to occur in the muscle groups held in the shortened position on the affected side, the patient may also demonstrate unnecessary muscle activity on the intact side. He may clench his fist, replicate the attempted movement, or stiffen his arm and leg, and this muscle activity must also be prevented if the patient is to develop motor control on his affected side.

It is possible that some therapeutic techniques in current use may encourage the development of recovering muscle activity into stereotyped synergies and actually prevent the patient from re-establishing the best possible motor control. Below are some illustrations of this theory.

### 1. Stimulation of Mass Movement Patterns

The Jacksonian theory that movement not muscles is represented in the motor cortex, which is no longer held to be correct,[10,15,16] has probably been responsible for the emphasis in the past 30 years being on the stimulation of 'movements' and away from eliciting activity in discrete muscles.

The suggestion that it is necessary to stimulate mass movements implies that human movement can be classified into relatively few 'patterns' of activity, when in reality movement is infinitely complex and variable. For example, the patterns of movement described by Knott and Voss[17] may take into account the anatomical arrangements of muscles but the movements are stereotyped and bear little resemblance to the complexities involved in performing motor tasks.

It is preferable to train muscle activity within the specific context in which it occurs, that is, taking into account such details as the range of movement, leverage, the effect of gravity and the fact that each muscle has several component parts which are recruited in different synergies at different times.[18] For example, in lying, when the arm is taken from the side to above the head, muscle activity changes in response to the arm's changing relationship to gravity. In performing this activity normally, muscle work changes from concentric in one group to eccentric in the opposite group, and the ability to make this shift is essential for control and function (see Fig. 2.16b). However, resistance to this movement will encourage the use of one group of muscles concentrically throughout the entire range of movement. Similarly, if a person lying with his arm flexed at 90° to his body takes his hand to touch his face, the triceps brachii will normally need to contract eccentrically, i.e. to lengthen. If the therapist gives resistance to the patient's attempts at touching his head, she is encouraging him, as in the former example, to activate the incorrect muscles for accomplishing the goal by himself. This may reinforce the tendency to develop overactivity in the flexors of the upper limb.

Stimulation of mass movements has been suggested as a means of eliciting or facilitating a motor response, with the intention that these movements can then be refined as the patient regains motor function.[13] The problem is, however, that if a highly diffuse muscular pattern is used in this way, it is *this* pattern which will become learned. The diffuse pattern will then have to be eliminated by practice later on. It is preferable for the patient to receive more specific training, i.e. to be trained to contract specific muscles within the context of specific tasks in order that these tasks can be relearned.

### 2. Resisted Exercise

There is no evidence that activation of increasing numbers of motor units will alone produce any improvement in motor control in the brain-damaged person. Norton and Sahrmann[19] postulate that use of resistive techniques may decrease the ability of the patient both to activate muscles selectively and to cease muscle activity once initiated. They also suggest that unnecessary voluntary effort, at various stages during walking for example, may be a major contribution to walking dysfunction.

Since certain muscles demonstrate activity more obviously than other muscles in the early stage following stroke, resisted exercises tend to be directed towards these muscles. Hence, shortened, potentially 'spastic' or overactive muscles may be exercised to the exclusion of their antagonists, reinforcing the disabling muscular imbalance and contracture so typical following stroke.

### 3. Encouragement of Movement of the Intact Side to Assist the Affected Side

When the therapist encourages the patient to move his affected leg by using his intact leg, for example in getting out of bed, or to pivot on his intact leg when standing up—manoeuvres which the patient is frequently taught in the belief that they will enable him to achieve some level of independence—she is in fact encouraging compensatory behaviour which could have a negative effect upon his potential recovery of real independence. In being trained to replace use of his affected limb with use of his intact limb, he is learning *not* to use the affected side ('learned non-use').[20] It is possible that this emphasis on the intact side will cause interhemispheric interference, resulting in an 'extinction' of motor function of the affected side. Furthermore, use of the intact limbs, particularly when associated with effort, results in muscle activity in the affected limbs, but only in the most active (and usually the shortened) muscles. Hence, these manoeuvres will encourage a disabling muscle imbalance which will eventually lead to muscle contracture.

### PREVENTION OF MUSCLE IMBALANCE

To use the MRP in such a way as to enable the patient to recover effective function without disabling muscle imbalance and contracture, the therapist must appreciate the need to detect and train the patient to eliminate all muscle activity which is unnecessary to the movement or function being relearned. This includes the recognition and prevention of stereotyped and abnormal synergic activity even when it is relatively minimal and not grossly evident.

From the earliest stages of rehabilitation, the physiotherapist should ensure that motor activity is appropriate, and this requires an understanding of normal muscle function in specific motor tasks. When the patient contracts incorrect muscles for a task, he should receive immediate verbal feedback from the therapist, who points out his error. The patient needs to understand that it is by 'turning down' or 'turning off' muscles not required in the movement that he will learn how to 'turn on' the correct ones. Therefore, the therapist will point out to him not only where muscular activity is incorrect, but also when it is unnecessary. It is in this way that the therapist prevents muscle imbalance from developing, prevents 'learned non-use' of the affected limbs through overuse of the intact limbs, and enables the patient to regain motor control.

It is important not to confuse elimination of unnecessary activity with a generalised relaxation. It seems important in learning a task (that is, in the cognitive phase of learning a motor skill) that the person is mentally and physically 'ready' for action. Sometimes, some preparatory muscular activity is necessary to set the scene, so that the nervous system is not having to make a shift from an inactive to an active state. In pointing out unnecessary muscular activity to a patient who is practising a particular function, the therapist should not encourage a general relaxation but a turning down or off of a particular muscle or muscle group which is interfering with effective performance of the task.

Weight-bearing through the affected leg in standing has been suggested to have an inhibiting effect upon the development of extensor overactivity. However, there may be another explanation of the importance of weight-bearing. If a patient practises bearing weight through his affected leg while moving about in standing (and stretches his calf in sitting) from the earliest days following his stroke, he is less likely to develop contractures of his calf muscles and hip flexor muscles. Standing bearing weight through the limb involves hip extension. Since hip extension takes place in standing by angular displacement at the ankle as well as the hip, the calf muscles as well as hip flexors are lengthened, and, because the hip is slightly forward of the knee, knee extensor muscle activity need only be minimal. It may be that the prevention of shortening of hip flexor and calf muscles in this way also prevents the 'extensor' (plantarflexor and knee extensor) overactivity so commonly reported in stroke patients who stand with weight principally through the intact leg.

The Programme also suggests ways of preserving length in the finger, wrist and elbow flexors, which develop contractures very quickly because of the resting posture of the upper limb. Once the patient has regained some active control over his wrist and finger extensors, passive means of maintaining muscle length are no longer necessary.

Contracture has been shown to be an important factor in functional capability following central neurological lesions in animals[21] and in humans.[22] Perry and colleagues comment that increasing spasticity and deformity (as reported by Twitchell[23]) during the early weeks following stroke may well demonstrate the influence of contracture formation rather than neural change.[24]

## REFERENCES

1. Denny-Brown D. and Botterell E. H. (1948). The motor functions of the agranular frontal cortex. *A. Res. Nerv. & Ment. Dis. Proc;* **27**:235.
2. Perry J. (1980). Rehabilitation of spasticity. In *Spasticity: Disordered Motor Control* (Feldman R. G., Young R. R. and Werner K. P., eds), pp.87–99. Chicago: Year Book Medical.
3. Basmajian J. V. (1976). Electromyographic investigation of spasticity and muscle spasm. *Physiotherapy;* **62**:319–23.
4. O'Connell A. L. (1972). *Understanding the Scientific Basis for Human Movement.* Baltimore: Williams and Wilkins.
5. Bruner J. S. (1973). Organisation of early skilled action. *Child Develop;* **44(4)**:1–11.

6. Broer M. R. and Zernicke R. F. (1979). *Efficiency of Human Movement*, 4th edn. Philadelphia: W. B. Saunders.
7. Blomfield S. and Marr D. (1970). How the cerebellum may be used. *Nature*; **227**:1224–8.
8. MacConaill M. A. and Basmajian J. V. (1969). *Muscles and Movements. Basis for Human Kinesiology*. Baltimore: Williams and Wilkins.
9. Kottke F. J., Halpern D., Easton J., Ozel A. and Burrill C. (1978). The training of co-ordination. *Arch phys. Med*; **59(12)**:567.
10. Basmajian J. V., ed. (1978). *Muscles Alive: Their Functions Revealed by Electromyography*, 4th edn. Baltimore: Williams and Wilkins.
11. Taub E. and Berman A. J. (1968). Movement learning in the absence of sensory feedback. In *The Neuropsychology of Spatially Oriented Behavior* (Freedman S. J., ed.) pp.173–192. Illinois: Dorsey Press.
12. Riddock G. and Buzzard E. F. (1921). Reflex movements and postural reactions in quadriplegia, with special references to those of the upper limb. *Brain*; **44**:397.
13. Brunnstrom S. (1970). *Movement Therapy in Hemiplegia*. New York: Harper and Row.
14. Walsh F. M. R. (1923). Certain tonic or postural reflexes in hemiplegia with special reference to the so-called 'associated movements'. *Brain*; **1(46)**:1–37.
15. Eyzaguirre C. and Fidone S. J. (1975). *Physiology of the Nervous System*. Chicago: Year Book.
16. Phillips C. G. (1978). In laying the ghost of 'muscle versus ligaments', a lecture to the Xth Congress of Neurological Science. In *Muscles Alive; Their Functions Revealed by Electromyography*, 4th edn (Basmajian J. V., ed.) p. 107. Baltimore: Williams and Wilkins.
17. Knott M. and Voss D. E. (1968). *Proprioceptive Neuromuscular Facilitation*, 2nd edn. New York: Harper and Row.
18. Basmajian J. V. (1977). Motor learning and control: a working hypothesis. *Arch. Phys. Med. Rehabil*; **58**:38–41.
19. Norton B. J. and Sahrmann S. A. (1978). Reflex and voluntary electromyographic activity in patients with hemiparesis. *Phys. Ther*; **58**:951–5.
20. Taub E. (1980). Somato-sensory deafferentation research with monkeys: implications for rehabilitation medicine. In *Behavioral Psychology in Rehabilitation Medicine: Clinical Applications* (Ince L. P., ed.) pp. 371–401. Baltimore: Williams and Wilkins.
21. Travis A. M. and Woolsey C. W. (1955). Motor performance of monkeys after bilateral, partial and total cerebral decortications. *Brain*; **78**:273.
22. Herman R. (1970). The myotatic reflex—clinico-physiological aspects of spasticity and contracture. *Brain*; **93**:273–312.
23. Twitchell T. E. (1951). The restoration of motor function following hemiplegia in man. *Brain*; **74**:443.
24. Perry J., Giovan P., Harris L. J., Montgomery J. and Azaria M. (1978). The determinants of muscle action in the hemiparetic lower extremity. *Clin. Orthopaed. Related Res*; **131**:71–89.

# Appendix 3

# Feedback

Feedback gives information about the environment and our place within it. It gives us knowledge of performance and knowledge of results. It is derived from external sources via the eyes, ears and skin, and from internal sources via proprioceptors and labyrinths. The term feedback is, however, also used to describe the generation of information within the brain itself, without direct reference to the periphery. It is considered that this may allow for monitoring of movement, by a comparison between the intended motor output and the appropriate motor programme.

Kelso and Stelmach[1] categorise three types of feedback which are important in the modulation of movement as: (a) response feedback, in which information is received as a direct result of muscle contraction; (b) external feedback, where information is received from the environment, usually in relation to a goal and as an indirect result of muscle contraction; and (c) internal feedback, or information generated prior to the response from structures within the nervous system.

**The relative importance of the various receptors to movement** and to the learning of movement is the subject of some controversy. The exact roles in motor control of muscle spindle[2,3] and Golgi tendon organ[4-6] and of the joint receptors[7-9] are not yet understood and results from studies remain conflicting. This situation reflects the complex nature of movement control.

It is possible that the emphasis which has been placed in physiotherapy on the primacy of tactile and proprioceptive inflow may be misplaced.[10-14] Bizzi and Polit[15] comment that the proprioceptors have an uncertain role in the execution of voluntary movements. Taub and Berman[13] point out that although proprioceptive feedback may accompany movement, this does not mean it is essential to that movement. Jones[11] suggests that methods of physiotherapy to improve motor control may be ineffective if based solely on the theory that proprioceptive feedback is essential to movement.

The theory that somatosensory feedback is essential to movement was based largely on the work of Mott and Sherrington,[16] who showed in experiments with monkeys that, following complete deafferentation of one limb, the limb was in effect paralysed. The theory which developed from this was that tactile and proprioceptive impulses are essential for movement, that there could be no effective movement without such feedback.

However, several researchers, in particular Taub and his colleagues, have shown in their experiments with monkeys that following unilateral deafferentation, similar to that used in the original work by Mott and Sherrington, the animals can be induced to use the limb by training techniques and techniques to increase motivation, although the deafferented animals needed more time to learn new tasks than the intact animals.[17] Furthermore, when monkeys are bilaterally deafferented,[13,18] following an immediate postoperative period when the limbs are useless, the animals are capable of using the limbs effectively for a wide variety of functions, without training, although they often lack the fluency of control and of precise timing found in intact animals.

The data from deafferentation experiments have been used to provide support for the theories of **central control of movement**. Evarts,[19] for example, points out that when sensory feedback is eliminated by deafferentation, it is interesting to see the extent to which new movements can be learned on the basis of knowledge of results and internal feedback. These studies and others imply that although sensory feedback is probably necessary for the fine tuning of movement, many motor programmes are genetically endowed, and the relationship between peripheral feedback and movement is not as simple as is implied by a sensorimotor dichotomy.

It may be that the central nervous system has a considerable amount of autonomy and independence from the periphery in the acquisition and maintenance of motor skill. The theory of internal feedback loops suggests that, once a motor skill is learned, the brain monitors its own efferent outflow, checking it against the appropriate motor programme.

In the last two decades, there has been a proliferation of theories regarding the role of central nervous system neurons in motor control. Terms such as feedforward,[20–23] efference copy,[24] corollary discharge[25–27] and central efferent monitoring[19,28,29] have been used in an attempt to explain the mechanisms which underly motor organisation. Miles and Evarts[30] discuss certain aspects of these motor organisation theories in an attempt to organise the data.

Herman[31] has suggested that the central nervous system appears to process and integrate spatial and temporal information which is derived from: (a) an intrinsic, centrally controlled sensori-motor loop which elicits signals of intended movement (central efferent monitoring), which could be called 'sense of innervation'; and (b) an extrinsic, peripherally controlled loop which elicits signals of actual movement, which could be called 'sense of performance'. Herman sums up the situation in this way: '. . . performance can be effectively controlled by the intrinsic system although external feedback may be continually required to distinguish finer levels of motor outflow discharges and to systematise information regarding the relationship between the two systems'.

Although the processes which underlie movement are not understood, it is frequently proposed that the central nervous system may be capable of generating and monitoring its own motor output, although somatosensory feedback is necessary at certain stages of motor learning and for certain motor acts if they are to be performed with a fine degree of accuracy. The most recent interpretation of the anatomical findings regarding central and peripheral nervous systems is thus that some movements are made under preprogrammed, central (open loop) control, while others are made under peripheral (closed loop) control. This view is probably a response to the inadequacies of both the central and peripheral approaches.[32]

It has recently been pointed out by Reed[32] that it is no longer valid to assume that 'afferent' corresponds to 'sensory' and 'efferent' to 'motor'. Motor commands, for example, are both afferent and efferent. This raises the issue of a more ecological approach to motor behaviour which is in distinction to the traditional mechanistic physiology of reactions. The reader is referred to Reed's article for elaboration of this matter.

It is important to be aware of the controversies surrounding motor control, as prognostic significance has been attached to sensory deficiencies following stroke, patients with somatosensory dysfunction being considered to do poorly in rehabilitation. Unfortunately, this assumption will result in a negative attitude towards such a patient.

It is probable that physiotherapists have not placed sufficient emphasis on, or perhaps realised the significance of, verbal feedback (particularly in relation to knowledge of performance) and visual feedback (for knowledge of results) to the learning of motor control. Many studies have pointed out the relationship of vision to the acquisition and control of movement.[15,33,34] Other studies[11,35] have indicated that techniques of augmenting proprioceptive input such as resistance have little effect on accuracy of movement if verbal or visual knowledge of result is eliminated. The reader is referred to J. J. Gibson's work on vision as a means of gaining information about the environment which is critical to the performance of motor tasks.

It is the authors' experience that proprioceptive and tactile deficiencies are not necessarily indicators of poor prognosis following stroke. Poor results in rehabilitation and persistence of sensory dysfunction may be due instead to a failure of therapists to implement appropriate motor training techniques. It may be that the patient, like any person learning to control a motor activity, will learn effective movement again if he has a clearly identified goal, and if knowledge of performance and of results,[36-38] via vision, hearing (auditory feedback) and manual guidance, is accurately and continually given to him by the therapist and if motivation is stimulated.

Experience with the MRP indicates that proprioceptive, tactile and vestibular deficiencies gradually improve as therapy progresses, movement training itself apparently improving the patient's sensory perception. Movement is considered to be a vital factor in the brain's ability to adapt to visual, auditory, tactile and proprioceptive disturbance,[39-41] and the MRP gives the patient early and active experience of familiar everyday tasks with emphasis on using the affected limbs. Treatment techniques which emphasise the intact limbs and do not give early practice of standing and early task-specific training of motor control in affected limbs probably augment and perpetuate disordered perception of sensation.

The following points about feedback should be kept in mind throughout the various sections of the MRP.

1. The patient is encouraged to use **visual information** to give him knowledge of performance and knowledge of results, and to provide him with spatial cues and to encourage scanning. This enables him to anticipate and predict any environmental change. He may need to be reminded to watch what he is doing, particularly with activities involving the hands. He is given the opportunity to compare his performance as he 'senses' it internally with what he looks like when he sees a videotape of himself, or when he compares his performance of the task with the therapist's demonstration. He can be encouraged to use a vertical reference point with which to line himself up. A patient with homonymous hemianopia may need to be reminded to turn his head to compensate for his deficit. However, specific visual defects related to stroke should be given special training.

2. The therapist gives **verbal feedback, as part of training**, monitoring the patient's performance so he knows whether or not it is correct, at what point the movement goes wrong, at what point inappropriate muscle activity is interfering with the movement. She also proposes strategies for improving his next attempt. With very specific and accurate verbal feedback, patients following stroke can learn to recognise, isolate and produce fine degrees of neuromuscular activity.[31]

One segment of the MRP can be used as an example. In walking, one movement component to be learned is flexion of the knee at the start of swing phase, that is, with the hip in extension. This is practised in prone lying (see p. 141). Initially, the patient may only be able to contract his knee flexors spasmodically and in their inner range. The therapist feeds back to him information about muscle contraction immediately it occurs, getting him to practise eccentric and concentric movement in the small range he *can* control, gradually increasing this range. Early in practice, verbal feedback needs to be instantaneous. As soon as the patient starts to lose control over the flexors, he should move back to the point where he has control, then gradually attempt to maintain that control over an increasing range of movement. The therapist must ensure that the patient can make the transition from concentric activity as he flexes his knee to eccentric activity as his leg is lowered into extension, and all of this activity must be monitored verbally to the patient as he moves. Counting is an effective way of receiving feedback about the length of time a muscle contraction can be maintained, and it provides motivation.

This example illustrates what is probably a most important factor in the learning of movement. As Herman[31] has pointed out, motor control may be induced by providing a precise and reliable signal regarding the required function, and the signal must provide information about the action with respect to the initiation, the execution and the termination of the action—and this without delay. The patient seems more readily able to learn the task if this information (by verbal feedback and manual guidance) is continued throughout his attempts at eliciting a controlled movement. As he develops control, the type of feedback and guidance change.

**Verbal feedback is used carefully for reinforcement**. Only a successful performance, not merely a good attempt, is rewarded by 'Good', so the patient knows exactly what he must repeat. An unsuccessful performance should elicit from the therapist 'No, that's not right yet—next time don't move your other leg'.

Another important verbal technique in the MRP is the explanation to the patient of his problem, the strategy for overcoming it, that is, what he is to practise and why. For him to practise a component of a task such as flexion of the knee for swing phase of walking, he must have as complete an understanding as possible of the importance of this component, and of the muscles he must activate in order to walk. By understanding the problem he is working on, the patient is able to make the best use of the verbal feedback he receives from the therapist as he practises controlling knee flexion and as he uses this newly acquired control in walking.

Patients are frequently able to improve motor control with an explanation, a clearly identified and specific goal, and verbal feedback as the only 'techniques' used by the therapist. Unfortunately, some patients with communication problems will have difficulty with verbal techniques and these techniques must be replaced by non-verbal instruction and demonstrations, and by feedback given by gestures, photographs, or videotapes. A patient with left brain damage in particular may do better if verbal instructions are given **before** he attempts the task, not while he is performing it, as one process may interfere with the other.[42]

Other authors have expressed the view that the brain-damaged person would relearn more effective motor control if he received feedback as described above, and some have pointed out that physical therapy is usually deficient in this regard.[31] They have suggested, therefore, what is variously described as augmented feedback, sensory feedback, biological feedback therapy or biofeedback,[43–45] as a means of achieving this objective. Although, at the present time, biofeedback is mostly used where other methods of treatment have failed, or in conjunction with inappropriate and even conflicting methods of physiotherapy, it provides a useful adjunct to the MRP because the Programme provides a specific analysis of motor problems and a guide to the muscles which need to be retrained for specific tasks. The limb load monitor has been used in conjunction with the standing sections in the Programme.

Biofeedback will no doubt be more effectively used in future rehabilitation. However, the value of feedback given by a skilled therapist, who understands normal movement and muscle action and who can analyse the patient's movement problems accurately and feed the appropriate information back to him, cannot be overemphasised. Biofeedback should be developed as a tool to give the patient visual and auditory feedback of muscle activity when it is not perceptible to palpation or vision, and to enable the patient to undergo periods of monitored practice when the therapist is unavailable, and for practice, with the therapist, of certain movement components or aspects of motor control with which he is having particular difficulty.

## REFERENCES

1. Kelso J. A. S. and Stelmach G. E. (1976). Central and peripheral mechanisms in motor control. In *Motor Control: Issues and Trends* (Stelmach G. E., ed.) New York: Academic Press.
2. Bizzi E., Polit A. and Morasso P. (1976). Mechanisms underlying achievement of final head position. *J. Neurophysiol*; 39:435–44.
3. Kelso J. A. (1977). Motor control mechanisms underlying human movement reproduction. *J. Experimental Psychology: Human Perception and Performance*; 3:529–43(b).
4. Gelfand S. and Carter S. (1967). Muscle sense in man. *Exp. Neurol*; 18:469–73.
5. Goodwin G. M., McCloskey D. I. and Matthews P. B. C. (1972). The contribution of muscle afferents to kinaesthesia shown by vibration-induced illusions of movement and by the effects of paralysing joint afferents. *Brain*; 95:705–748.
6. Matthews P. B. C. (1980). Developing views on the muscle spindle. In *Progress in Clinical Neurophysiology*, Vol. 8 (Desmedt J. E., ed.) pp. 12–27. Basel: Karger.
7. Skoglund S. (1973). Joint receptors and kinaesthesis. In *Handbook of Sensory Physiology: Somatosensory System 1* (Iggo I., ed.) pp. 111–136. Berlin: Springer.
8. Marteniuk R. G. (1979). Motor skill performance and learning: considerations for rehabilitation. *Physiotherapy Canada*; 31:4.
9. Roy E. A. and Williams I. D. (1979). Memory for location and extent: the influence of reduction of joint feedback information. In *Psychology of Motor Behaviour and Sport* (Roberts G. C., Newell K. M., eds.) Illinois: Human Kinetics Publishers.
10. Jones B. (1972). Outflow and inflow in movement duplication. *Perception and Psychophysics*; 12:95.
11. Jones B. (1974). The importance of memory traces of motor efferent discharge for learning skilled movements. *Develop. Med. Child Neurology*; 16:620–28.
12. Lashley K. S. (1964). *Brain Mechanisms and Intelligence*. New York: Hafner.
13. Taub E. and Berman A. J. (1968). Movement learning in the absence of sensory feedback. In *The Neuropsychology of Spatially Oriented Behaviour* (Freedman S. J., ed.) pp. 173–192. Illinois: Dorsey Press.
14. Stelmach G. E. (1968). The accuracy of reproducing target positions under various tensions. *Psychonomic Science*; 13: 287.
15. Bizzi E. and Polit A. (1979). Characteristics of the motor programs underlying visually evoked movements. In *Posture and Movement* (Talbott R. E. and Humphrey D. R., eds.) pp. 169–176. New York: Raven Press.
16. Mott F. W. and Sherrington C. S. (1895). Experiments upon the influence of sensory nerves upon movements and nutrition of the limbs. *Proc. Roy. Soc. London*; 57:481–8.
17. Taub E. (1976). Motor behavior following deafferentation in the developing and motorically mature monkeys. In *Neural Control of Locomotion* (Herman R. et al., eds.) pp. 675–705. New York: Plenum Press.
18. Taub E. (1980). Somatosensory deafferentation research with monkeys: implications for rehabilitation medicine. In *Behavioral Psychology in Rehabili-*

*tation Medicine: Clinical Implications* (Ince L. P., ed.) pp. 371–401. Baltimore: Williams and Wilkins.

19. Evarts E. V. (1971). Feedback and corollary discharge: a merging of the concepts. *Neurosciences Research Project Bulletin;* **9**:86–112.
20. MacKay D. M. (1966). Cerebral organisation and the conscious control of action. In *Brain and Conscious Learning* (Eccles J. C., ed.) pp. 422–445. New York: Springer.
21. Ito M. (1974). The control mechanisms of cerebellar motor systems. In *The Neurosciences Third Study Program* (Schmitt F. O. and Worden F. G., eds.) pp. 293–303. Cambridge, Mass: MIT Press.
22. Kornhuber H. H. (1974). Cerebral cortex, cerebellum and basal ganglia: An introduction to their motor function. In *The Neurosciences Third Study Program* (Schmitt F. O. and Worden F. G., eds.) pp. 267–80. Cambridge, Mass: MIT Press.
23. Teuber H. L. (1974). Key problems in the programming of movements. *Brain Res;* **71**:533–68.
24. Von Holst E. (1954). Relations between the central nervous system and peripheral organs. *Brit. J. anim. Behav;* **2**:89
25. Sperry R. W. (1950). Neural basis of the spontaneous optokinetic response produced by visual inversion. *J. Comp. physiol. Psychol;* **43**:482–9.
26. Teuber H. L. (1964). The riddle of frontal lobe function in man. In *The Frontal Granular Cortex and Behaviour* (Warren J. M. and Akert K., eds.) pp. 410–444. New York: McGraw Hill.
27. Kennedy D. and Davis W. J. (1977). Organisation of invertebrate motor systems. *Handb. Physiol;* **1**:1023–87.
28. Oscarsson O. (1970). Functional organisation of spino-cerebellar paths. In *Handbook of Sensory Physiology 2* (Iggo A., ed.) pp. 121–127. Berlin: Springer.
29. Bruner J. S. (1973). Organisation of early skilled action. *Child Development;* **44,4**:1–11.
30. Miles F. A. and Evarts E. V. (1979). Concepts of motor organisation. *Ann. Rev. Psychol;* **30**:327–62.
31. Herman R. (1973). Augmented sensory feedback in the control of limb movement. In *Neural Organisation and its Relevance to Prosthetics, Symposia Specialists;* **73–82041**: 197–212.
32. Reed E. S. (1982). An outline of a theory of action systems. *J. Motor Behav;* **14** (2): 98–134.
33. Smyth M. M. (1978). Attention to visual feedback and motor learning. *Journal of Motor Behaviour;* **10**:185–90.
34. Adams J. A., Gopher D. and Lintern G. (1977). Effects of visual and proprioceptive feedback on motor learning. *J. exp. Psychol;* **9**:11–22.
35. William I. D. and Stelmach G. E. (1968). The accuracy of reproducing target positions under various tensions. *Psychonomic Science;* **13**:287.
36. Gentile A. M. (1972). A working model of skill acquisition with application to teaching. *Quest;* **17**:3–23.
37. Marteniuk R. G. (1976). *Information Processing in Motor Skills.* New York: Holt, Rinehart and Winston.
38. Wallace S. A. and Hagler R. W. (1979). Knowledge of performance and the learning of a closed motor skill. *Res. Quart;* **50,2**:265–71.
39. Held R. (1965). Plasticity in sensory motor systems. *Scientific American;* **213**:84–94.
40. Luria A. R. (1961). *The Role of Speech in the Regulation of Normal and Abnormal Behaviour.* Oxford: Pergamon.
41. Greenwald A. G. (1970). Sensory feedback mechanism in performance con-

trol: with special reference to ideo-motor mechanism. *Psychol. Rev;* **77**:73–99.

42. Stockmeyer S. (1981). Interference and Co-operation in Hemispheric Function. Unpublished paper given at *First Austral-Asian Physiotherapy Congress, Singapore.*

43. Brudny J., Korein J., Grynbaum B. and Sachs-Frankel G. (1977). Sensory feedback therapy in patients with brain insult. *Scand. J. Rehab. Med;* **9**:155–63.

44. Gonella C., Kalish R. and Hale G. (1978). A commentary on electromyographic feedback in physical therapy. *Phys. Ther;* **58**:11–14.

45. Kelly J. L., Baker M. P. and Wolf S. L. (1979). Procedures for E. M. G. biofeedback training in involved upper extremities of hemiplegic patients. *Phys. Ther;* **59,12**:1500–1507.

## FURTHER READING

Gallistel C. R. (1980). *The Organization of Action. A New Synthesis.* Hillsdale, New Jersey: Erlbaum.

Reed E. and Jones R. (eds) (1982). *Reasons for Realism. Selected Essays of James J. Gibson.* Hillsdale, New Jersey: Erlbaum.

# Appendix 4

# Practice

Practice is known to be a necessary prerequisite for acquiring skill in motor performance. Practice without any other consideration, however, is not necessarily effective, nor will it necessarily result in learning. For example, without feedback as to its accuracy or otherwise, practice may actually prevent the learning of skill. Some factors which must be considered if practice is to be effective in rehabilitation are outlined below.

## GOAL IDENTIFICATION

Learning a complex motor task involves two major components: identifying what is to be learned and organising the information in the correct sequence to carry out the task. The patient must be aware of the goal for which he is practising and the goal must be readily identifiable as one which he considers important. The goal should be short term, that is, capable of fulfilment on the day of practice, although it will be directly related to another, longer term, goal. For example, the short-term goal may be to straighten the hip in standing; the longer term goal would be to stand alone or to walk independently.

A goal should, at all stages of the patient's rehabilitation, be reasonably hard yet attainable. This usually produces a better performance than a goal which is too easy or too general.[1] When the patient is practising with the therapist, he should experience success, even if at first his performance needs substantial manual guidance and monitoring from the therapist. He should not repeatedly experience failure. He should finish each therapy session with the feeling that he has been practising successfully and that he will continue to be successful with less and less guidance. As soon as he has some control over a task, the therapist adds increasing complexity to what he is practising or slightly varies the task by increasing the environmental demands. For example, the patient's goal may be to stand erect and make the necessary postural adjustments as he reaches forward with one arm. Once he can achieve this, even though not 100% of the time or with 100% accuracy, the therapist suggests a new goal. The patient now has to reach sideways and then behind him without moving his feet. Although he has a different goal, in fact he is still practising making postural adjustments, but the therapist has added variety to the task.

Variety and complexity can also be added by changing the rhythm or the timing of a movement. Practising in this way should enable the patient to push his optimum performance continually higher. A major fault in much therapy is that the patient spends time practising what he can already do. As Taub[2] suggests, it is important that when the patient is ready he moves on, as practising at the same level of performance may actually impede progress.

Similarly, the goal can be changed, the timing or rhythm altered, in order to make a task possible if the patient is having difficulty practising without error. To go back to the above example, if the patient is having difficulty making postural adjustments, and is making too many errors, the therapist may change the goal, asking the patient to turn and look over his shoulder while he thinks about keeping his hips extended and in front of his ankles. Note that it is only the short-term goal which has changed. Analysis of the reasons for his difficulty has enabled the therapist to determine the action to be taken. It would have been incorrect to assume that standing is too difficult for the patient and to postpone the goal of standing in favour of some activity in sitting.

## RELEVANCE OF PRACTICE

The patient must be able to see the immediate relevance of what he is practising to the functions he wants to perform. However, in much present-day rehabilitation, the patient practises what is not directly relevant, for example leg and trunk exercises on his back, exercises on the floor, exercises for his intact side and gross movement patterns for his limbs and trunk.[3-5] Such exercises do not convey to the learner the dynamic components which are necessary if he is to perform those everyday functions which he must learn.[6] Rehabilitation should be more directly related to everyday life. The theory in physiotherapy has been that the performance or practice of exercises is eventually generalisable into the everyday motor tasks which the patient cannot perform. For example, strengthening exercises given to the legs with the patient in supine, or walking on the knees will improve the patient's ability to walk—the former because muscle strength is generalisable into many different activities, the latter because it is easier to practise with a lower centre of gravity than in standing.

The theoretical assumptions underlying these concepts are, however, no longer tenable. It is now accepted (although it has been slow to reach the field of rehabilitation) that training should be task and context specific. New theoretical assumptions are now being made based on evidence from the field of movement science. Walking on the knees is not likely to generalise into improved walking on the feet since the muscle activity learned for one task is inappropriate for the other. Not only are the muscles used for one task different to those used in the other, but so also are the relationships of muscles to each other, the lengths of contracting muscles, and the associated postural adjustments.

The MRP consists of modules of everyday motor tasks in which the patient is specifically trained for what he needs to learn. Practice sessions are organised to simulate real-life situations and make the adjustment from the therapeutic session to everyday life relatively easy.

Even at the muscle level, the training of activity must be relevant to the task.[7] If the patient has difficulty contracting his knee extensors when weight-bearing through the leg (i.e. in 0–15° in standing or during the stance phase of walking), he will not learn to control them specifically for this activity by practising full-range knee extension. He may learn to contract his knee extensors in their outer and middle range but still be unable to control the necessary 0–15° of knee movement when bearing weight in standing (i.e. with the foot as a fixed point). Instead, the patient needs to practise concentric and eccentric knee extensor activity in the 0–15° range (see p. 136).

Similarly, it may be possible to elicit foot dorsiflexion in sitting (i.e. with hip and knee flexed) but the patient may find it impossible to dorsiflex his foot on heel strike (i.e. with hip flexed and knee extended). The patient should practise ankle dorsiflexion in a manner which is relevant to what is required for heel strike in walking (see Fig. 8.19, p. 144). Practice must therefore take into account the specific task and the context in which it is being performed.

Practice should seem logical to the patient, the various steps following each other in a systematic order. He needs to understand what he is doing. Throughout each part of the MRP, the patient should see the logical sequence of what he is practising now in terms of what he will do next. If the material is well organised, he will be able to use this information to solve similar motor problems. There is a greater transference of training when preparatory activities contain components identical to those required for the performance of the skill itself.[6]

## Open and Closed Skills

Poulton[8] used the terms open and closed to make a distinction between the environmental demands of tasks. Open tasks refer to those that require adaptation of movements to events in the environment, and closed tasks refer to those that can be carried out without reference to the environment. Gentile[9] suggests that effective teaching to improve skill in motor performance requires analysis of the nature of the environmental demands of the task to be learned. The authors consider that this has implications for therapy intervention. For example, training of standing up from the same firm surface in the physiotherapy area is to train it as a closed skill, in which the environmental conditions are fixed, stable and stationary. The patient, however, needs to be able to stand up from a variety of surfaces and under different environmental conditions; that is, both the spatial and temporal characteristics of motor performance need to be matched to the spatial and temporal characteristics of the environment. In order to develop this flexibility, the patient needs to practise the task under different environmental conditions. The reader should refer to Gentile[9,10] for further discussion on open and closed tasks.

## WHOLE OR PART PRACTICE

It is generally considered that motor acts can be taught in their entirety or broken down into their component parts.[1] Which is the better method has been discussed in the literature on motor learning in relation to non-brain-damaged people.[11,12] Although it may be sufficient for the stroke patient to practise an entire activity, such as standing up from a chair, it is often necessary for him to practise some component of the activity with which he is having particular difficulty. He may need to practise contracting a specific muscle at a particular length. Practice of the component is followed immediately by practice of the entire activity. Using the example of standing up, the patient may need to practise inclining his extended trunk forward at his hips and pushing down through his feet in order to get his centre of gravity appropriately placed for standing up. This constitutes practice of a component. He must then practise standing up from the chair, concentrating on the component he has just practised. He should have the opportunity to repeat the practice of any component he finds difficult whenever necessary and whenever unwanted movement habits are retarding progress.

## ATTENTIVENESS

Initially, the patient may have difficulty isolating the muscle action required, or a particular component in an activity. He will need to be reminded to concentrate and be attentive to what he is doing. If too much information is given to him, he may pay attention to what is irrelevant. Clinically, inattentiveness or misdirected attention is found to limit the effectiveness of practice, and Diller[13] reports that improved performance has been found to be associated with improved attention.

The therapist should make an active attempt to engage in eye contact while within relatively close range of the patient, as this not only aids concentration but also orientation in space. Furthermore, it is a means of communicating positive attitudes[14] and helps create a bond between therapist and patient.

Practice of moving about in sitting seems to foster the ability to pay attention and to concentrate. Early success in such an activity, particularly in a patient whose first attempts at any movement resulted in failure, may be a significant factor in improving concentration. Improved concentration may also be due to the regaining of movement control in a position which enables the patient to re-orient himself with his surroundings. The sitting position also fosters eye contact and communication with staff and relatives.

## CUES

Different cues are probably more important at different stages of learning.[1,15] Fitts[16] suggested three stages in learning a skill—cognitive, associative and automatic. The patient seems often to respond best in early recovery to more cognitive cues. However, once he has developed some motor control he may respond better to more automatic ones. One of the objectives of practice is to enable him to make the transition from the cognitive stage to the automatic stage.

Verbal and visual cues appear to be essential in the early stages of learning. What the therapist says to the patient before and during practice constitutes an important **verbal cue**, and instructions and explanations need to be very direct and explicit in order to trigger off the desired motor behaviour. For example, 'Move your bottom back and sit down' may be more effective in initiating hip and knee flexion with weight shift backwards than 'Sit down' or 'Bend your knees and hips'.

Sometimes, in order to elicit the desired behaviour, the therapist may need to give the patient a different goal (by verbal cue or instruction), although the overall goal remains the same. For example, if the therapist is teaching the patient to extend his hip in lying so he can stand with his hips extended, she may ask him to contract his hip extensors (see Fig. 7.6b). If he cannot do this, she gives him another goal (i.e. changes the verbal cue), which would have the same result, asking him to push his heel down towards the floor, thus directing his attention away from the specific muscle activity. When he is successful, she takes him back to his former goal, pointing out that he has in fact achieved what she had originally asked.

The therapist must take care not to give so lengthy an instruction that the patient does not know at what part of the sentence to direct his attention. She should ensure, for example, that the essential verbal cue does not come at the end of a long sentence, by which time a patient who is having difficulty concentrating will have stopped listening. Similarly, she should not distract a patient who is having difficulty shifting from one topic to another by introducing irrelevant information. She should also take care to avoid information overload.

**Visual cues** are important, for directing and correcting movement and for making postural adjustments (refer to Appendix 5). The eyes give information on position in space and position relative to other objects. For example, the patient reaches towards the therapist's hand, or turns to look behind him. The therapist must be prepared to guide and encourage eye movement just as she would guide and encourage other movements. Many stroke patients, particularly those with right brain damage, have great difficulty initially in directing their gaze to the appropriate place and keeping it there.

Used discretely, **tactile cues** will reinforce verbal instruction. However, persistent tactile stimulation will distract the patient's attention from the activity he is practising. It is important to reduce all tactile stimuli to the most essential[13] so the patient can concentrate only on the cues which are relevant. That is, the most essential cues should not be lost amidst a variety of different ones. If the patient has tactile inattention (extinction), it is particularly important that tactile stimulation to the intact side is minimal until he has been trained to overcome his tendency to extinguish the stimulus on the affected side.

## ERRORS IN PRACTICE

Although the opportunity to make some errors in the execution of movements is probably beneficial for learning,[17] persistent incorrect practice of a task will retard progress, as the patient will, at a later stage, have to unlearn the incorrect movements in order to learn the activity correctly. Errors, if they are practised and become well learned, interfere with subsequent attempts at making a correct response. It is known that if an athlete practises a motor task incorrectly, he will have to spend considerable time inhibiting and unlearning the abnormal movement in order to be able to perform it more efficiently.[18] The stroke patient will have even greater difficulty because of his tendency to develop the wrong emphasis in movement and also because it will usually be too frustrating and complex for him to learn to move in a different manner once he has learned incorrectly. Consequently, if, for example, the patient practises walking with a three- or four-point cane *this* behaviour will become learned and it is unlikely that he will be motivated to unlearn this pattern later and learn to walk more efficiently. If he has a low expectation of his motor potential, he may no longer *want* to make the change. Lack of success in rehabilitation may well stem from a failure to understand the long-term ineffectiveness of the false 'independence' which results from a compensation with the intact side at the expense of recovery of the affected side.

Unfortunately, compensation with the intact side may reinforce another problem, what Taub[2] calls 'learned non-use'. In the example given above, the patient who learns to walk with a four point cane will not take weight normally through his affected leg and, because he does not *need* to use this leg correctly in this type of walking, he will learn *not* to. Clinically it is very apparent that, although a person may, if he is motivated to do so, be able to unlearn an incorrect movement and learn to perform it correctly, it is usually impossible to overcome 'learned non-use' of a limb, probably due to secondary perceptual dysfunction.

## PATIENT PARTICIPATION

The patient must be encouraged and shown how to develop a problem-solving attitude to practice by questioning his performance, comparing it to normal and correcting errors when they occur. He should work with the therapist in evaluating his performance and learn from her his major problems and the strategies which he can use to overcome them. He needs to know why he fails and why he succeeds and what solutions are available for overcoming error. He should **actively** participate and not just have things done to him and for him.

**Mental practice** or **task rehearsal**[19-22] appears to be helpful to some patients in learning particular movements and can be used even before the person has regained the ability to elicit active muscle contraction. For specific periods of time during the day, the patient thinks through a movement, visualising the entire movement in his mind. As with physical practice, mental practice should be performed without gross error. As this is difficult to monitor, the therapist should ensure that the patient knows what he should practise. Visual cues are considered to be the most useful aids to mental practice.[22]

## MANAGEMENT OF PRACTICE

Practice is a continuum, ranging from overt practice to covert (mental) practice.[23] Although the most meaningful and effective training sessions for the stroke patient will be those he spends with his therapist, it is important to **plan a programme** of practice for the rest of the day, as actual physical therapy sessions will occupy only a small part of the 24 hours. The need for consistency throughout the day, with the patient having the opportunity to practise particular tasks alone and with other members of the staff, has been discussed elsewhere in this book.

The type of practice, whether covert or overt, and the duration and frequency of practice sessions will vary depending on the patient's level of skill and the goal. Frequency, intensity and duration of training are of key importance in any programme to improve the efficiency and effectiveness of motor performance. Repetition of near-peak performance is considered to be necessary for the development of movement control,[3] but how often and for how long is unclear. Furthermore, moderate overload of muscle is necessary to develop strength and to increase cardiopulmonary endurance. However, an important aspect to consider in planning the practice sessions will be the provision of clear visual or written instructions about the goals and a means of gaining information about performance. **Videotape**[24] and **photographs** can provide the patient with an illustration of skilled performance of a task, the opportunity to see his own attempts and a way of checking up on his mental practice. A study by Gonnella *et al.*[6] demonstrated that self-instruction using an audiovisual medium was effective in enabling normal subjects to learn a new skill. The hypothesis that subjects could learn the cognitive aspects of the motor task in one viewing of a film was supported, and transfer of learning to the physical performance of the task was found to occur. This finding has clinical implications for stroke patients.

**Written instructions** can provide the specific goals to be practised and suggestions about the frequency and distribution of practice sessions. These instructions should be written down by the patient himself or by the therapist and will need updating regularly. A performance chart or checklist which the patient uses to monitor his performance can also be provided by the therapist. This list will also be helpful for other staff and relatives. Some form of learning curve or self-reports will provide feedback and motivation.

## FATIGUE

The therapist need not assume that the patient, because he has had a stroke or because he is elderly, will tire easily during practice. If he appears to be fatigued, or complains of fatigue, the possible reasons for this must be considered. It may be that he is having too much sedation or that his vital capacity is reduced. The activities he is expected to practise may be too difficult, in which case he may appear 'unco-operative', or too easy, in which case he becomes bored and dispirited. He may not be able to see the immediate relevance of what he is practising. It is interesting that the patient who is experiencing success during therapy sessions and whose programme enables him to move on from one task to the next, seldom complains of fatigue. The normal fatigue which accompanies physical activity will respond to a period of rest, and fatigue within normal limits does not affect learning, although it may temporarily affect performance.[25-27]

After the patient has been practising a particular task for a period of time, the resultant fatigue is probably related to one or other of the following factors: (a) mental—the necessity to concentrate hard on a particular action; and (b) physical—the muscle activity necessary to maintain a position and to move. It is more effective in terms of the patient's need to learn if he is given another activity to practise rather than given a 'rest'. A different activity will require different muscle work and a different goal on which to concentrate. It seems necessary to keep up the person's level of alertness and to transfer the alertness developed in one activity to another activity. It was found in studies with normal subjects[28,29] that the amount of muscle work which could be performed after a 'diverting activity' was always greater than the amount of muscle work which could be performed after a passive pause. One study with a small group of patients[30] indicates that this may also be so following stroke.

## REFERENCES

1. Singer R. N. (1980). *Motor Learning and Human Performance*, 3rd edn. New York: Macmillan.
2. Taub E. (1980). Somatosensory deafferentation research with monkeys: implications for rehabilitation medicine. In *Behavioral Psychology in Rehabilitation Medicine: Clinical Application* (Ince L. P., ed.) pp. 371-401. Baltimore: Williams and Wilkins.
3. Brunnstrom S. (1970). *Movement Therapy in Hemiplegia*. New York: Harper and Row.
4. Knott M. and Voss D. E. (1968). *Proprioceptive Neuromuscular Facilitation*, 2nd edn. New York: Harper and Row.
5. Johnstone M. (1978). *Restoration of Motor Function in the Stroke Patient*. London: Churchill Livingstone.

6. Gonnella C., Hale G., Ionta M. and Perry J. C. (1981). Self-instruction in a perceptual motor skill. *Phys. Ther*; **61**:177–84.

7. Basmajian J. V. (1977). Motor learning and control: a working hypothesis. *Arch. phys. Med*; **58**:38–41.

8. Poulton E. C. (1957). On prediction in skilled movement. *Psychol. Bull*; **54**:467–78.

9. Gentile A. M. (1972). A working model of skill acquisition with application to teaching. *Quest*; **17**:3–23.

10. Gentile A. M., Higgins J. R., Miller E. A. and Rosen D. M. (1975). The structure of motor tasks. *Mouvement;* **7**:11–28.

11. Naylor J. C. and Briggs C. E. (1963). Long-term retention of learned skills: A review of the literature. *ASD Technical Report* **61**–390. US Department of Commerce.

12. Fitts P. M. and Posner M. I. (1967). *Human Performance*. Belmont, California: Brooks/Cole.

13. Diller L. (1970). Psychomotor and vocational rehabilitation. In *Behavioral Change in Cerebrovascular Disease* (Benton A. L., ed.) pp. 81–116. New York: Harper and Row.

14. Mehrabian A. (1969). Significance of posture and position in the communication of attitude and status relationships. *Psychol. Bull*; **71**:359–72.

15. Leithwood K. A. and Fowler W. (1971). Complex motor learning in four-year olds. *Child Develop*; **42**:781–92.

16. Fitts P. M. (1964). Perceptual motor skill learning. In *Categories of Human Learning* (Melton A. W., ed.) pp. 243–286. New York: Academic Press.

17. Newell K. M. (1981). Skill learning. In *Human Skills* (Holding D. H., ed), pp. 203–26. New York: John Wiley & Sons.

18. Lawther J. D. (1977). *The Learning and Performance of Physical Skills*, 2nd edn. Englewood Cliffs, New Jersey: Prentice Hall.

19. Jacobsen E. (1932). Muscular phenomenon during imagining. *Amer. J. Psychol*; **49**:677–94.

20. Jones G. J. (1965). Motor learning without demonstration of physical practice, under two conditions of mental practice. *Res. Quart*; **36**:270–76.

21. Cardinall N. (1977). Mental practice. Unpublished paper delivered at *53rd Congress of APTA, St Louis, Missouri.*

22. Johnson P. (1984). The acquisition of skill. In *The Psychology of Human Movement* (Smyth M. and Wing A. M., eds), pp. 215–40. New York: Academic Press.

23. Leiper C., Miller A., Lang J. and Herman R. (1981). Sensory feedback for head control in cerebral palsy. *Phys. Ther*; **61**:512–18.

24. Del Rey P. (1971). The effects of video-taped feedback on form accuracy and latency in an open and closed environment. *J. Motor Behavior*; **3**:281–7.

25. Marteniuk R. G. (1979). Motor skill performance and learning: considerations for rehabilitation. *Physiotherapy Canada*; **31**:187–202.

26. Bilodeau E. A. (1952). Massing and spacing phenomena as functions of prolonged and extended practice. *J. exp. Psychol*; **44**:108–13.

27. Cochran B. J. (1975). Effect of physical fatigue on learning to perform a novel motor task. *Res. Quart*; **46**:243–249.

28. Asmussen E. and Mazin B. (1978). A central nervous component in local muscular fatigue. *Europ. J. appl. Physiol*; **38**:9–15.

29. Asmussen E. and Mazin B. (1978). Recuperation after muscle fatigue by 'diverting activities'. *Europ. J. appl. Physiol*; **38**:1–7.

30. Chaco J., Blank A. and Gonen B. (1981). Recovery after muscular fatigue in hemiparesis. *Amer. J. phys. Med*; **60**:30–32.

# Appendix 5

# Adjustments to gravity

The human body is perpetually submitted to the force of gravity. The whole motor system is organised towards either counteracting or utilising the effects of this force. We can only discount the force of gravity when we are lying down or sitting with the body fully supported. Holt[1] comments that, because it cannot be seen, we sometimes forget the effect of gravity on everything we do.

The **force of gravity** is always exerted in a vertical direction downwards towards the centre of the earth. The line which passes from the centre of gravity of the mass towards the centre of the earth is known as the **line of gravity**. A mass is said to be balanced when its **centre of gravity** is positioned over the base of support and the centre of gravity is the point about which the mass balances, that is, the point at which the weight of the mass can be considered to be controlled. In general, it is said that the centre of gravity of the body is in the region of the hips.[2] (Under static conditions it is estimated that the centre of gravity lies just anterior to the second sacral vertebra.[3]) The human body consists of segments which are constantly moving and different in shape from each other. The 'shape' of the human body is constantly changing during movement, and its centre of gravity will therefore also change.

The **ability to maintain an upright position** (i.e. a posture) involves some postural adjustments to protect the stability of the body. These movements are **automatic** and in general the subject is unaware of them. Usually they are adjustments of the body segments on one another and do not move the body from one position to another. These adjustments generally involve muscular activity throughout the body even though the adjustments may be slight, and Martin[4] comments that they are in keeping with the principles of mechanics.

All self-initiated and imposed movements require postural adjustment. When a subject is moving from one position to another, for example standing up, he may be conscious of the activity and the purpose of the activity yet throughout the act there are postural adjustments of which he remains unaware. Reaching or pointing requires postural adjustments because of the alteration in the centre of gravity which results from the arm movement. These postural adjustments are both anticipatory and ongoing.[5] Furthermore, they appear to be strongly linked to the task and to the context in which the task is performed.

Standing is associated with **postural sway**, which involves little muscular activity. When the subject is standing at ease, postural sway is only slight. Herman[6] states that 'the ability of man to stand with little expenditure of neuromuscular energy is due to the tensile strength of ligaments and muscles, the mechanical features of some joints and the compensatory changes of the centre of gravity of body segments.' He goes on, 'the control of balance in posture is to provide intermittent correction of balance rather than steady antigravitational control'. To allow for normal body sway in standing without loss of balance, weight should fall near the centre of the base, between the feet and in front of the ankles. The most efficient base in standing is with the feet a few inches apart, as they are when the legs are vertical. This gives as large a base as possible without introducing a diagonal force against the ground.

In simple terms, **postural adjustments keep the body segments appropriately aligned.** Efficient balance requires correct timing and muscular control in order to maintain alignment. If a body segment is out of line with the segment(s) below, the bones and the joints are out of line, tension of the opposing ligaments is unbalanced and excessive muscle tension is required to prevent loss of balance. Normally, balance is maintained with a minimum of strain when each segment is centred over the one below, i.e. normally aligned.

However, **body segments are constantly moving**. Whenever a segment moves, there is an adjustment of the body. Postural adjustments have been observed even during movements of the thoracic walls during respiration. When a body part moves away from the line of gravity in one direction, there is a shift in the centre of gravity in the same direction. Another segment must therefore move in the opposite direction. If the arms are lifted forward to shoulder level, the centre of gravity is now further forward and upward within the body, and the adjustment of the body must therefore be backwards. Just how great the adjustment is depends on the weight of the arms, the distance they are moved and the speed of the movement. The actual adjustments made are dependent upon the goal of the task.

If the line of gravity falls outside the base and appropriate adjustment can no longer be made, a new base directly below the centre of gravity must be established. In other words, balance is lost at this point until a new base is established. **Loss of balance**, therefore, occurs when the person is unable to compensate and to preserve balance. At this point the limbs are extended to absorb the impact (protective support), that is, one steps forward or puts out one's hand for support.

In the last few decades there has been much research into postural adjustments which is particularly relevant to physiotherapy and which should allow an extensive updating of our clinical practice. The following are some major factors with clinical implications arising from research findings.

**Postural adjustments and movements** are not distinct and dichotomous in terms of both control and behaviour, but are **highly**

**interdependent.** Several authors have proposed that postural support is a component of volitional movement of the limbs.[7-9]

**Postural adjustments are both preparatory (anticipatory) and ongoing.** Belen'kii and colleagues[10] showed that movement of the arm in standing is accompanied by reactive moments of force in the whole kinematic chain. They suggested that the preparatory muscle activity which occurred before the motor act began set the mechanical parameters of muscles and therefore the kinematic links of the body in advance of the perturbation. This minimises the perturbation and, hence, energy expenditure. Similar findings have since been reported by others.[9,11]

The interrelationship between postural adjustments and focal movements (such as reaching in standing) seems to vary from one context to another (or from one task to another). That is, **postural adjustments** could be said to be **task specific.**[12]

Nashner[13] has proposed that this interrelationship between postural and focal muscles varies systematically with the conditions of support. His experiments with subjects standing on a movable platform and holding a handle have shown that those muscles acting on the most stable support (either arm muscles or leg muscles) may be preferentially activated.

Other experiments[14] have shown that the temporal order of muscle activation changes in different contexts. In unexpected perturbations, muscle activity begins distally and works proximally. However, in tasks which are intended to be destabilising, muscle activity occurs first around proximal joints.

**Balance is not merely a response to a stimulus but rather an interaction with the environment.** It has been suggested that the intelligent organism selects the information it needs in order to achieve current goals rather than just responding to stimuli.[15] It has been shown experimentally that a reflex response can be overriden in a situation in which it would be destabilising.[16] Hence, although there are situations in life in which there is no intentional movement but merely movement in response to environmental perturbation (on a boat or train), it is probably reasonable at this point to assume that postural adjustments, whether anticipatory or concurrent, are actually part of the functional synergy involved in the particular motor task and therefore become efficient as part of the learning of that particular task.

**Vision and its role in balance** has been investigated by Lee, who has proposed that visual information is 'exproprioceptive', since it gives us information about our position relative to the environment. His experiments and those of others[17-19] have shown that visual information overrides proprioceptive information from muscles and joints under certain circumstances.

Theories and research into the role of vision in action have been significant in the developing interest in the interaction between organism and environment. It has been proposed that perception and the organism's ongoing interaction with the environment cannot be separated. Emphasis is thus placed on the organism as 'active' and 'information seeking'.[18]

**Balance training** should therefore not be considered as separate from training of everyday tasks. Balance is dynamic, it is never static, and balance training should enable the learner to regain the dynamic components necessary for each individual function. Balance may, in other words, be improved without direct training, being acquired dynamically as part of the practice of a task.[20]

Much physiotherapy for balance dysfunction has encouraged the patient as a responder to perturbations initiated by the therapist. Current therapy for patients with balance dysfunction could be said to fall into two categories—facilitation therapy and exercise therapy. The facilitation therapy model consists of two methods based on differing assumptions about control mechanisms. 'Rhythmic stabilisations', developed by Knott and Voss[21] as part of their proprioceptive neuromuscular facilitation (PNF) regimen, was designed principally to improve 'stability'. 'Facilitation of automatic postural reactions' (specifically equilibrium and righting reactions) was developed by Bobath[22] to improve the underlying background to movement as represented by the postural reflex mechanism. The exercise therapy model was designed to elicit muscle activity and strengthen muscles and may involve the patient practising on a balance board.

These models were based on certain theoretical assumptions of the first half of this century and hence need to be re-examined in the light of the knowledge of the 1980s. The facilitation therapy model, for example, is based on the concept of balance adjustments occurring in response to external perturbations and fails to consider the need for anticipatory and ongoing postural adjustments forming part of self-initiated motor tasks. In this Programme an attempt has been made to develop training methods which would enable a patient to regain an active and information-seeking role.

Certain points about the training of motor tasks need to be kept in mind:

1. The maintenance of stability in the upright position requires very little neuromuscular energy when body segments are aligned correctly. Emphasis in treatment is therefore on correcting alignment of body segments with a normal base of support during the performance of a series of tasks graded according to their destabilising effect.

2. Movement or displacement of any segment of the body is a source of disequilibrium because of the shift of the centre of gravity which must be accompanied by an appropriate adjustment of posture. The patient learns to make these adjustments himself as he moves from one position to another or as he reaches, points etc., the therapist monitoring his alignment. This builds up his confidence in his own abilities.

3. The retraining of balance in sitting and standing requires that the patient experience these positions. That is, he will not regain the ability to stand until he is in the standing position. It should be noted that the regaining of balance control in sitting is not a prerequisite for standing. The alignment of the body segments to each other in sitting and standing is different and the biomechanics (and therefore the muscle activity) are also different. It is important to recognise the fact that the patient will

only regain good control over balance in either position if he practises in that position. Several studies have indicated that balance is highly specific in terms of particular activities and positions.[12]

4. During treatment, the therapist must ensure that she does not position herself too closely to the patient or hold him in such a way that she will prevent postural adjustments or render them unnecessary.

## REFERENCES

1. Holt K. S., ed. (1975). How and why children move. In *Movement and Child Development*, pp. 1–7. Philadelphia: W. B. Saunders.
2. Broer M. R. and Zernicke R. F. (1979). *Efficiency of Human Movement,* 4th edn. Philadelphia: W. B. Saunders.
3. Saunders J. B., Inman V. T. and Eberhart H. D. (1953). The major determinant in normal and pathological gait. *J. Bone Jt Surg*; **35-A**:543–58.
4. Purdon Martin J. (1977). A short essay on posture and movement, *J. Neurol. Neurosurg. Psychiat*; **40**:25–9.
5. Massion J. and Gahery Y. (1979). Diagonal stance in quadrupeds: a postural support for movement. In *Progress in Brain Research*, 50 (Granit R. and Pompeiano O., eds.) pp. 219–26. Amsterdam: Elsevier/North Holland Biomedical Press.
6. Herman R. (1976). Postural control and therapeutic implications. In *Advances in Orthotics* (Murdoch G., ed.) pp. 471–483. London: Edward Arnold.
7. Higgins J. R. (1972). Movements to match environmental demands. *Res. Quart*; **43**:3123–36.
8. Turvey M. T., Shaw R. E. and Mace W. (1978). Issues in the theory of action: degrees of freedom, coordinative structures and coalitions. In *Attention and Performance*, VII (Requin J., ed.), pp. 557–95. Hillsdale, New Jersey: Erlbaum.
9. Lee W. A. (1980) Anticipatory control of postural and task muscles during rapid arm flexion. *J. Motor Behav*; **12** (3):185–96.
10. Belen'kii V. Ye., Gurfinkel V. S. and Paltsev Ye. I. (1967). Elements of control of voluntary movements. *Biophysics*; **12**:135–41.
11. Weiss P. L. and Hayes K. C. (1979). *Postural Control Mechanisms*. Proceedings 4th Congress of ISEK, Boston, Mass.
12. Lawther J. D. (1977). *The Learning and Performance of Physical Skills*, 2nd edn. Englewood Cliffs, New Jersey: Prentice Hall.
13. Nashner L. M. (1982). Adaptation of human movement to altered environments. *Trends Neurosci*; **5**:358–61.
14. Nashner L. M. and Cordo P. J. (1981). Relation of automatic postural responses and reaction-time in voluntary movements of human leg muscle. *Exp. Brain Res*; **43**:395–405.
15. Arbib M. A. (1981). Perceptual structures and distributed motor control. In *Handbook of Physiology*. (Brooks V., ed.), pp. 1449–80. Bethesda, Maryland: American Physiological Society.
16. Nashner L. M. (1976). Adapting reflexes controlling the human posture. *Exp. Brain Res*; **26**:59–72.
17. Lee D. N. and Aronson E. (1974). Visual proprioceptive control of standing in human infants. *Percep. Psychophys*; **15**:529–32.
18. Lee D. N. and Lishman J. R. (1975). Visual proprioceptive control of stance. *J. Hum. Movement Stud*; **1**:87–95.

19. Dietz V. and Noth J. (1978). Preinnervation and stretch responses of triceps brachii in man falling with and without visual control. *Brain Res;* **142**:576–9.

20. Gonella C., Hale G., Ionta M. and Perry J. C. (1981). Self-instruction in a perceptual motor skill. *Phys. Ther;* **61**:177–84.

21. Knott M. and Voss D. E. (1968). *Proprioceptive Neuromuscular Facilitation.* New York: Harper & Row.

22. Bobath B. (1985). *Abnormal Reflex Activity*, 3rd edn. London: Heinemann Medical.

# Index

185